Stability

How an ancient monastic practice
can restore our relationships, churches,
and communities

Nathan Oates

PARACLETE PRESS
Brewster, Massachusetts

2021 First Printing

Stability: How an Ancient Monastic Practice Can Restore Our Relationships, Churches, and Communities

Copyright © 2021 by Nathan Oates

ISBN 978-1-64060-546-6

Library of Congress Cataloging-in-Publication Data
Names: Oates, Nathan, author.
Title: Stability : how an ancient monastic practice can restore our
  relationships, churches, and communities / Nathan Oates.
Description: Brewster, Massachusetts : Paraclete Press, 2021. | Summary:
  "Oates explains the ancient Benedictine vow of stability, which he believes can
  remedy the destructive influence of consumerism in our times"– Provided by publisher.
Identifiers: LCCN 2021015163 (print) | LCCN 2021015164 (ebook) | ISBN
  9781640605466 (trade paperback) | ISBN 9781640605473 (epub) | ISBN
  9781640605480 (pdf)
Subjects: LCSH: Benedictines–Spiritual life. | Monastic and religious
  life. | Vow of stability. | Choice of church. | BISAC: RELIGION /
  Christian Living / Calling & Vocation | RELIGION / Christian Living /
  Spiritual Growth
Classification: LCC BX3003 .O27 2021 (print) | LCC BX3003 (ebook) | DDC
  255/.106–dc23
LC record available at https://lccn.loc.gov/2021015163
LC ebook record available at https://lccn.loc.gov/2021015164

10 9 8 7 6 5 4 3 2 1

Published by Paraclete Press
Brewster, Massachusetts
www.paracletepress.com

Printed in the United States of America

Contents

With love to my wife, Carmen, and our three children,
Sienna, Isaiah, and Matthias.
May your roots grow deep
and may you experience the fruit of stability.

A True Story

A t 1:15 a.m. on March 27, 1996, twenty members of the Armed Islamic Group of Algeria (GIA) stormed the quiet Abbey of Our Lady of Atlas monastery of Tibhirine, in the Médéa Province of the North African country, kidnapping seven French Trappist monks at gunpoint.[1]

For decades the region, indeed the whole country, had been terrorized by escalating conflict between the Algerian government and various violent rival Islamic groups. The 1990s in Algeria were dominated by indiscriminate, chaotic, and brutal violence. Car bombings targeting schools, municipal buildings, and cafes became so frequent that the government banned parked cars in the city of Algiers. Fake highway check points became sites of random, brutal killings. Stories published nearly weekly throughout the '90s in the *Wall Street Journal* and the *San Francisco Chronicle* relayed harrowing accounts of armed assailants slitting the throats of farmers in their fields, abducting young girls in broad daylight, and hooded men with axes raiding weddings. In 1995 alone, more than 3,000 people were killed amidst the violent conflicts which virtually paralyzed the country in fear.[2]

The monastery in the mountains above the village of Tibhirine seemed to shield the locals from the ever-encroaching violence. Villagers spoke of the "monastic effect."[3] In stark contrast to the surrounding areas, there had been no theft or violence in the tiny town at the foot of the mountain. Perhaps it was the practical benefits of the monastery's dispensary and Dr. Luc, one of the monks, who offered free medical care to nearly one hundred people a day. Others believed an influential Islamic leader had extended his protection to the monks out of respect for their leader.[4] The monks knew their presence was somehow critically linked to the security of the village. However, within a few minutes on March 27, 1996, both the monks and the peace of the monastery were ripped away.

In his book *The Monks of Tibhirine* John Kiser describes the monks' abduction with chilling simplicity:

> Brother Jean-Pierre was woken by voices outside his gatehouse room, which faced onto the passageway leading from the exterior court into the cloister. At that time of night, he thought the commotion had to do with [those] wanting [Dr.] Luc's services. . . . From behind the curtains of his glass door, he could see a man with a turban, bandoliers, and a machine gun walking toward the room of [the other monks]. Jean-Pierre stepped back and listened. He could hear someone give the order to open the exterior gates. A few minutes later, there was the sound of footsteps shuffling past his front door. The outside gate clanged shut. A dead silence followed.[5]

It wouldn't be until sunrise that Jean-Pierre and Amédée, the only two monks to escape the notice of the kidnappers, felt they could accept the risk of leaving the monastery in order to report the abduction of their brothers to the police. Tragically, three weeks later, when the French president and his foreign minister announced they were unwilling to negotiate with the GIA, all seven monks were martyred.

The story of the monks of Tibhirine is also beautifully told in the 2010 French film *Of Gods and Men*. Against the backdrop of the imminent violence surrounding the monastery, the story's real conflict, as depicted in the movie, is whether the monks should stay at the monastery in Tibhirine or leave for the safety of their mother house in France. The film's power is delivered through intimate scenes in which the monks struggle to come to terms with their calling to the place and its people, and labor to discern a faithful and wise response to their call.

The real power of the monks' stable presence in Médéa is revealed in a scene which takes place in the tiny kitchen of one of the homes near the monastery.[6] Family members are discussing with a few of the monks the news of recent violence at the town market. It's at this point that one of the monks confesses, "We may be leaving." To which one of the village leaders responds, "Why are you leaving?" After a long pause, another monk explains, "We are like birds on a branch. We don't know if we will leave." The next to speak is a woman, who says simply and directly, "We're the birds; you're the branch. If you go, we lose our footing."

Introduction

This is a book about becoming that *footing*.

This is a book about changing culture by *staying*.

And this is a book about *how stability births meaningful movement.*

Much of the movement happening in our always-mobile culture is destructive, resulting in frenzied individuals, disintegrated families, fractured communities, and toxic environments. The engine of this destructive movement is the well-nourished desire for gratification through consumption. Often aimless and self-centered, this destructive movement is little more than a repeating cycle of leaving and looking. But some of the movement happening among us is powerfully effective. It grounds us personally, enriches our relationships, restores environments. This restorative movement is deeply rooted and others-focused. It is the result of staying and finding.

The distinction between the two kinds of movement is this: one seeks to get (to acquire, to consume), while the other aims to give (to serve, heal, restore). The secret of the kind of movement that restores is that *it is the fruit of having not moved for a long time.*

Movement that matters is borne out of authentic stability. Only those who have stayed long enough to know themselves and their mission can restore the broken world as they go. They become missionaries carrying hope. The rest are wanderers who are still searching for it. So, the basic message is *Go! Change the world. Restore the broken.* But first, stay. For in staying one practices the skills, lives the commitment, and learns the value of stability. And stability is what makes going count. Stability is what leads to movement that matters: movement that heals and does not harm, movement that is good, the kind of movement that restores all things.

What Is Stability?

As North American culture continues to shift in ways that challenge the once-favored position and perspectives of the church, Christians must discover and perhaps recover faithful ways of being the body of Christ in the world. Simply riding the wave of cultural influence by means of political and material power is no longer viable. We must learn to be the church in a time when the value of the church and her message is seen with skepticism, if not entirely dismissed. We must recommit to learning how to be the church in actual neighborhoods which need gospel-driven restoration displayed in clear and practical specificity.

The church has faced similar and far more severe situations before and has endured. For example, when the Roman Empire crumbled into ruins in the fifth century and threatened to destroy the Church in the process, a young monk from Nursia named Benedict emerged with a vision for Christian community which rescued not only the Church, but Western civilization as well. By looking to such examples from the past, we can reimagine effective ways of engaging the present and shaping the future. Failure to seriously consider the teachings and practices of those, like Benedict, who charted a faithful course through similarly challenging times is to ignore some of our greatest wisdom.

The fact that active and vibrant monastic communities still exist offers a compelling invitation to discover ways these ancient teachings are still being practiced. And the resurgence of new or "neo" monastic communities, intentionally embedding themselves in the fabric of their communities in twenty-first-century ways, reveals an essential element of meaningful cultural engagement. St. Benedict called this essential element "stability."

My hope is that this book will encourage you to engage the culture with a compelling alternative to the dominant values and practices of this culture. I invite you to consider, as one especially compelling alternative, the value of stability. I believe that by personally valuing and practicing stability, and by leading our churches toward becoming communities of stability, we will become an embodied force for restoration.

A Quick Roadmap

Here's where we're headed:

- I want to introduce you to man named Benedict.
- Then we'll talk about how God is not somewhere else: stability and God—the theology of stability.
- Then we'll talk about our restlessness and our need to not run: stability and self/soul.
- Next, we'll extend the discussion beyond ourselves to others: stability and meaningful relationships.
- Then we'll root the conversation in our specific contexts: stability and place.
- Ultimately, I want to explore how embracing stability is a means of restoring culture.
- And finally, I'll suggest specific stabilizing practices for today's church.

Why Me?

I'm not an expert on any of this, but this is what I'm learning.

In 2004, my wife and kids and I and a few good friends started a church in a small-but-growing northern California city. We've been sharing life and discovering Jesus in this place ever since. For the last ten years, I've been captivated by the connection between stability and social holiness, or to use different words, staying put as a strategy for the restoration of all things.[7] In the last two years, this fascination has taken me to Rome, where I lived for a few weeks with monks, to churches in Virginia and Michigan, where members live according to an adapted 1,500-year-old "Rule of life," to a 1.5 million-square-foot vertical village in Memphis where education and healthcare and small business and art and activism and development all take place under one roof . . . and to several other compelling examples of Christians restoring culture by staying.

I hope to simply share what I'm learning.

But . . . (An Objection or Two)

Last year, a colleague heard me speaking on this material and shared with me afterwards that he had a hard time navigating a few initial objections.

"Such as?" I asked.

"First, stability sounds boring."

"And second?"

"Monks seem irrelevant."

Fair enough. I acknowledge that consulting monks, who live their whole lives in one place, mostly secluded from the rest of the world, for insights into restoring our always-moving modern culture sounds, to some . . . strange.

But let me assure you of two things: First, there is a lot of life within those walls. Their life is deep and powerful and all-encompassing—definitely not boring. And second, while separation from much of what constitutes "real life" in the eyes of our culture may seem, at first, to invalidate their perspective, I would argue (with many others) that their separation is precisely what enables monks to see so clearly and speak so profoundly to our culture. In other words, monks are daily living a reality that most of us long for but rarely even taste.

By purposefully separating from the culture the monk does not forfeit his cultural relevance. It's part of what positions him to call the culture to health. Thomas Merton, the twentieth century's one famous American monk, once described monks as "trees that exist in obscure silence, but by their presence purify the air."[8]

If we will look and listen, we will realize that there is much to learn here about loving God and living life and—yes— restoring a broken world.

And while stability may never be the theme of a reality TV drama, many of us are, ultimately, captivated by the ability and willingness to stay. In the moment, stability may lack attraction. But in retrospect, as we consider the difference-makers, as we identify the most respected, as we celebrate the fifty-year marriages and the successful navigation of long-term challenges, the value of stability is revealed.

The answer to the question "What caused them to endure?" is compelling. If we are blessed to finally recognize the fruit of steadfast endurance, we will naturally ask, "What is at its root?" "What is the source of this significant impact?" "What is the foundation of work like this that lasts?" And what we will discover, beneath it all, is stability.

I offer this very brief definition of stability: it is the commitment to a purpose, a place, and a people. In an effort to arrive at a common language, here's a brief primer on "stability" from St. Benedict's Rule. The Latin, *stabilitas,* appears in the following six places in the Rule:

- 1:11 – (Speaking of what he called "gyrovagues," wandering monks without a fixed residence) "Always on the move, they never **settle down** (stabilitas), and are slaves to their own wills and gross appetites."
- 4:78[9] – "The workshop where we are to toil faithfully at all these tasks is the enclosure of the monastery and **stability** in the community."
- 58:9 – (Regarding the process of joining the monastic community) "If he promises to persevere in his **stability**, after a period of two months let this Rule be read to him straight through."
- 58:17 – (Regarding the Benedictine vows) "The one to be received, however, must first promise his **stability**, fidelity to the monastic lifestyle and obedience before all in the oratory."
- 60:9 – (Referring to clerics/priests who wish to join the monastery; the Latin literally says, "promise his stability," which doesn't translate well into English) ". . . but only if they too promise to observe the Rule and **stability**."
- 61:5 – (In the chapter on how visiting monks are to be received) "If he should later desire to promise **stability**, his wish should not be denied. After all, his way of life has become well known during his time as a guest."

Additionally, stability is clearly implied in the final line of the Prologue: "Never swerving from his instructions, then, but faithfully observing his teaching **in the monastery until death**, we may by patience share in the sufferings of Christ that we may deserve also to share in his kingdom. Amen."[10]

There is much more I'd like to say about all that. But first, I need to introduce you to someone.

Meet Saint Benedict

At a critical turning point in Western history, as the Roman Empire crumbled and fell, a young man named Benedict, from Nursia, Italy, built a series of small communities and a simple plan for the restoration of the Church. A few years earlier, disillusioned with the world of academia and the increasing moral decay of the church and society, Benedict dropped out of school and left Rome. He ventured into the wilderness, found himself a quiet cave by a river, and resolved to spend his life pursuing God in solitude and silence. But the solitude wouldn't last long. First a few, and eventually hundreds, of other young men found Benedict in the wilderness. They were seeking what could not be found in a culture which had collapsed and a church which had become corrupt: a humble, holy guide and a practical path to peace with God.

Thrust into leadership he did not seek, Benedict adapted the wisdom and practice of Eastern monasticism into a working structure which would shape the shared life of this new community. He eventually wrote a Rule of Life, a simple yet profound approach to a common life of prayer and work, and not without precedent at that time. Other early monastic leaders had done likewise, and Benedict borrowed some of their best ideas.[11] The golden thread that ran throughout Benedict's Rule was his unique contribution to the restoration of the Church and the culture: the value and the practice of stability.

Benedict is the father of Western monasticism. A quick tour through the history of monasticism begins with the desert fathers and mothers. These are mostly hermits living in total isolation. Then there's Egyptian and Eastern monasticism. These are loosely organized communities of hermits—like hermit suburbs. Each person has their own space, but they are clustered together.

Then Benedict is credited with moving monastic life into a fully shared communal experience. He set up multiple communities of twelve men and wrote a Rule for them to live by.

Benedict's work, known by its Latin name, "The Regula," or "The Rule of St. Benedict," was first written for the monks of Benedict's monastery in Monte Cassino. It was then picked up and used by others, including a monk named Gregory, who later became Pope Gregory the Great. Gregory wrote a powerful biography of Benedict which contributed to Benedict's Rule becoming the standard for Western monasticism by the late seventh century.[12] Today, Benedict is honored as one of the patron saints not only of Italy, but of all of Europe, because he is widely credited with saving Western civilization.

About ten years ago, I was in the library of a one-hundred-year-old retreat house on the California coast when I first saw a little red book on the shelf. Before that day I knew nothing about Benedict—nothing about the saint or the Rule. I put my finger on the top of the book, tilted it toward me, pulled it out, opened it up, skipped the introduction (which, by the way, is brilliant) and read the first sentence of the first chapter, which says, "There are clearly four kinds of monks."

There are? I thought. I was instantly intrigued. I kept reading and haven't stopped.

In addition to being personally enriched by this brief text, I have found it to be a surprisingly relevant source of wisdom for one navigating the challenges of modern pastoral leadership. In fact, I've discovered no greater help in leading a young church community.

Benedict's Frustration

What frustrated Benedict is what frustrates me still. He begins by defining four kinds of monks:

The Strong: In Benedict's view, the strong monk was the one who embraced a common life with a rule (a structured and balanced pattern of work and prayer) and an abbot (a spiritual leader). This was the ideal toward which he labored.[13]

The Hermits: Some monks, fortified by years of this kind of intentional communal experience, would enter into a life of solitude, ready, as he put it, "to fight against the devil" and "grapple single-handed with the vices of body and mind."

The Most Detestable: The third kind of monk Benedict called "the most detestable kind." These were those who did only as they pleased. Benedict writes, "Feigning devotion, their spirituality is a ruse. More like gypsies than true monks in their lifestyle, their character remains unformed." Caught up on their own "egoistic religious masquerade" they shared some level of community with those of like mind but remained "loyal to the world" and to their own whim.[14] They lacked any sign of obedience or stability.

The Even Worse: But the fourth kind of monks, which Benedict calls "gyrovagues" (a word he makes up that means they wander around aimlessly in circles). He says they are "in every way worse" than the third kind.

Apparently, in sixth-century Rome, there were people—try to imagine this—who would come to a faith community, be warmly welcomed as valued guests and offered hospitality, and they would be very enthusiastic about the community. "This is exactly what we've been looking for," they would say. "We are just so blessed to be here." But then, after a little while, when they were asked to participate in the shared work of the faith community, they would become critical, find something wrong with the worship or the music or the pastor or the practice of the community and they would leave. . . . And then they'd go to another faith community and the same thing would happen: They'd be warmly welcomed and honored and valued and they'd be all enthusiastic about it until they were asked to help and then they'd leave . . . (can you imagine this used to happen?) and the pattern would continue.

The Problem of Gyrovagues

Gyrovagues, Benedict writes, "spend their entire lives drifting from region to region, staying as guests for three or four days in different monasteries." The strategy here was to take full advantage of the generous Benedictine hospitality but to move on just before one was required to help with chores. (By the way, according to the Rule of St. Benedict, guests are to be welcomed as Christ . . . so these drifters would regularly receive spectacular hospitality, the best food, and an honored place at the table).

Benedict's indictment continues: "Always on the move, they never settle down, and are slaves to their own wills and gross appetites."[15]

These were the ultimate freeloaders. They avoided work, offered alibis, were always on the hunt for better offers, and feigned commitment to poverty in order to live as parasites. The gyrovague was a cultural dynamic that regularly impacted Benedict's church community. And he was quite frustrated about it.

In his first chapter Benedict identifies two behaviors which he finds destructive to faith communities. The first is hanging out with the few people you like best and agree with most and calling it Christian community. The second is when conflict arises, or you're asked to contribute or serve, or the shine wears off, you simply move on to something new and relatively easy. He says these kinds of behaviors are making a mockery of Christian community and the gospel. This is consumerism cloaked as Christianity.

I remember where I was sitting when I read these opening lines of the Rule for the first time, because I was astounded at the accuracy with which a sixth-century Italian monk described modern American Christian culture. And I thought: if this little book was written to address a sixth-century problem which is also a twenty-first-century problem, then perhaps his sixth-century solution could point the way toward the restoration of the church today. . . .

Benedict's Solution

What frustrated Benedict was rampant consumerism in the church. He was disgusted by a so-called Christianity that was, in reality, cloaked consumerism. Treating the church not as a community but as a commodity, taking and not giving, responding to challenges or conflict by leaving . . . these were the detestable patterns Benedict sought to make extinct.

What was Benedict's solution? Stability.

What Benedict required, in order to join his monastery, was that the person make three vows. Do you know what the first vow was . . . and still is? The vow of stability: the promise to seek God in this place with this community under the guidelines established by this rule.

To stay put.

Benedict's foundational response to the collapse of culture, the corruption of the church, and consumerism of the individual was the vow of stability. Other historic monastic communities emphasized vows of poverty or vows of obedience. Benedict is probably best known for emphasizing, as part of his vision for restoring church and culture, the vow of stability.

For example, in 2016, multiple earthquakes over a period of several weeks absolutely devastated the town where Benedict was born. Thousand-year-old churches crumbled. Houses collapsed. The water and power supplies were disrupted. Roads into town became impassable. Businesses closed. Thousands of people became homeless and most moved away.

Who stayed? The fifteen Benedictine monks. Why? Because they had made a vow of stability. In staying, not only did they demonstrate something fundamental about the character of God, but they literally became the foundation upon which the town's restoration began.

Three Layers and Three Images of Stability

Stability is, for Benedict, the most basic value of the spiritual life. He sees it as so valuable, in fact, that he makes the value a vow, and stability becomes the foundation on which he builds his "school for the Lord's service."[16] A clear modern definition of stability may be "a commitment to community."[17] But there's more to it than that.

At its root, stability is the blend of two biblical concepts: patient endurance and standing firm, which many appreciate in a general form and from a safe distance.[18] Benedict seeks to apply these biblical values more specifically. Benedict rescues the virtue, for which martyrs were so admired, from slipping into the archives of history. He makes fiercely practical the quality of character which both Saints Peter and Paul celebrate and encourage in the New Testament church.

For Benedict, stability has at least three layers.

Most practically, stability is remaining in a specific **place**—a specific monastery, with an abbot and a Rule—for one's entire life. The place is important not because of the place itself, but because of what staying in a specific place teaches and because of how it forms a person. That's the first layer.

Added to the layer of place are the **people** who share that space. Stability includes a commitment to sharing life and pursuing Jesus with others. It's the promise to contribute to the permanency of the people, specifically, and for the long term. It is not just the place or the people of that place, but the unique union of both people and place to which Benedict expects loyalty and responsibility.[19] To use a slightly different image, we could say that stability is the whole-hearted, lifelong commitment to both family and farm. Stability, for Benedict, is a fierce commitment not just to a place but to the community rooted in that place.

Finally, Benedictine stability includes a spiritual layer, a quality of devotion and contentment that, while forged in the physical realities of place and people, becomes less concerned about context and individuals and more focused on God's will as the "cell" or place in which the soul finds its rest. And this is critical, because the real problem stability addresses is the restless heart. We might begin to understand this layer as **purpose**.

Benedict was the first to make the vow of stability a requirement of entry into his monasteries. Why did he do this? What errors was he attempting to correct? Restlessness and consumerism. The widespread practice of the "wandering monk" in the fourth and fifth centuries was not too unlike the well-established American trend of "church hopping." Benedict recognized, as do many pastors today, the devastation caused to the church community and to the individual's soul by the unwillingness of so many to stay put.

So, we're going to learn from Benedict. In addition, the following three images may be helpful in getting a grasp of the value and practice of stability today.

Trees

The first song in the biblical book of Psalms begins,

Blessed is the one
> who does not walk in step with the wicked
or stand in the way that sinners take
> or sit in the company of mockers,
but whose delight is in the law of the LORD,
> and who meditates on his law day and night.
That person is **like a tree planted by streams of water**,
> which yields its fruit in season
and whose leaf does not wither—
> whatever they do prospers.

The central image of stability in the Bible is the image of a tree planted. It's an image that communicates strength (in contrast to brittleness), productivity (in contrast to bareness) and peaceful stillness (in contrast to chaos). In the Bible, the wisdom of the stable is contrasted with the fickle pursuits of the foolish. The blessed woman and the wise man are like trees planted, with deep roots and fruit-filled branches where others can find nourishment and rest. Stable people can be relied upon; they are trusted and respected, and they are loved.

Near our home in the suburbs is a small grove of 200-year-old oak trees. Occasionally we'll walk through them, admiring their weathered, majestic beauty. There is a weighty permanence to these old trees that stands in contrast to the fast-moving busyness that surrounds them. Like an old couple, married for fifty years, sitting in a room full of young singles looking for excitement, they're a bit bent over and worn down. But there's a deep contentment between them that everyone else is still searching for.

As we consider the wisdom of stability in the coming pages, one of the images we'll keep in mind is the image of a majestic oak tree rooted by streams of water.

Movement

A second image to keep close at hand in a discussion about stability is, perhaps surprisingly, the image of movement.

Have you noticed that the language that we often use to describe life *is* the language of movement? We're all moving through this journey called life. We are pilgrims on the way. We are passing through. We're rolling down the highway. She's cruising through life. He's over the hill.

On the surface a lot of movement looks pretty much the same. If you watch two different, random people board a plane, you witness nearly identical movement. Each person is doing almost exactly the same thing. If you watch two different young people pack up their cars and drive away from their childhood homes, their movement looks pretty much the same. But, in fact, there are two distinct kinds of movement. Simply stated, there is leaving and there is being sent.

In other words, there is aimless wandering . . . when you're not sure what you're even looking for. And there is walking with a purpose . . . when you're on your way to a specific destination with a clear intention. In one kind of movement, you're meandering. In the other kind of movement, you're on a mission. What's the difference? The meanderer is searching for meaning. The missionary has already found it. We'll dive deeper into the image of movement in the coming pages.

Pregnancy

A final image that brings clarity to the idea of stability is the image of a pregnant woman. This image beautifully combines the steadfast rootedness of the tree with intentional, purpose-driven movement.

The life being grown in the womb of a pregnant woman is literally rooted to her body. The placenta, through which the baby will receive her nutrients, is referred to by some birth professionals as the "tree of life"—both because of its function and because of its appearance.

So, there is powerful stability at work in the body of a pregnant woman. She is *with child*. The child is rooted to her mother. And this relational connection between woman and child is fixed, as if with a vow. Life, itself, is being shared relationally.

Moreover, the womb is a powerful example of stability to a place. It would sound ridiculous to apply our culturally influenced resistance to staying put in the same place to a baby in a womb. Because a womb is the very picture of contentment. The womb is enough. The womb is a place of stability. And it is a place of movement. There is both the movement of growth, development, and maturation that we naturally assume is happening in the womb. And there is the ultimate movement of birth from the womb into the world.

Though it is often difficult and marked by pain, we celebrate this movement of birth. This is what we've been anticipating! This is the goal of pregnancy and the great hope of the parent! The movement of birth gives life that changes the world.

Unless . . . the movement of birth happens too soon. We call this kind of birth *premature*. And we understand perfectly, in the context of pregnancy, a concept that seems to elude us in nearly every other sphere of life: life-giving movement follows a long season of stability. We recognize, in pregnancy, the true value and importance of a long season of stability. No efforts are made to shortcut this natural process. We protect this time as essential to future health. We see it as a time of critical nourishment and development of that life that is to come. Similarly, we celebrate the movement that comes from this time of pregnancy. We say, "The baby is ready to be born!"

Movement-as-birth was always the goal. What we understand in the image of the pregnant woman is the created order of things: healthy movement comes after a full season of staying put. Meaningful movement is rooted in stability.

CHAPTER 1
Stability and God
God is Not Somewhere Else

"The reason for stability?
God is not elsewhere."

—BYZANTINE LITURGY

I was surprised to hear that my friend was headed for California. We were sitting together at a camp in the Northwoods of Wisconsin where, for more than seven decades, thousands of people have testified to experiencing the presence of God. He planned to be one of them. But feeling disappointed, he was pursuing another experience in another place. He said he needed to go "somewhere else." "Why?" I asked. "To experience God" was his response. He hadn't in Wisconsin and was hoping to in California.

What saddened me about the exchange was his restlessness. Would he find what he claimed to seek by driving 2,000 miles west? I doubted it. Like a vagabond, he seemed drawn more to the road than the destination. His seeking felt more like wandering.

The Stability of God

The core theological flaw in his plan was this: God is not somewhere else. One of the core characteristics of God, according to the Bible, is that God is not limited to a specific location.

In the history of the people of Israel, God chooses to reveal God's self in a unique way: first, in the specific place of the tabernacle (which served as a sort of mobile sanctuary), and then in the temple (which became, for the Hebrew people, a permanent "house of God"). But even though God in a sense "dwelled" in the places, God was not limited to these places. God's power and God's presence existed and was experienced in other places.

So unlike the gods of other nations which were tied to specific regions or monuments or objects/idols, the God who was revealing himself to the world through the Hebrew people was the creator and ruler of everything. And this God was everywhere.

The theological word for this is "omnipresent." God is everywhere. God is always everywhere. One of the most beautiful—as well as one of the most challenging—ramifications of the Bible's assertion that God is omnipresent, or everywhere, is that God is always here.

Why is it a beautiful ramification? Because it means I can experience God wherever I go. Why is it a challenging ramification? Because it means God can be experienced right where I am. Right now. Right here.

Let's Start at the Beginning

The foundational biblical story of Abraham's grandson Jacob (who becomes the father of the twelve tribes of Israel), includes a scene in which Jacob is on the run. He's been manipulating the system and scheming for personal gain in a misguided attempt at grasping God's favor. Motivated by selfishness, he lies to his father and cheats his brother. Then he gets caught. But rather than repent, he runs.

Later, exhausted from running, he falls asleep on the side of the road and dreams about a stairway stretching from earth to heaven.

In the dream, God reveals his plan for Jacob and for the place where Jacob is. And Jacob's famous realization upon waking is this: Surely the LORD is in this place and I was not aware of it. Which sounds like a wonder-filled statement of praise, doesn't it? But it's not! Rather than joy, it's fear that grips Jacob's heart. Genesis 28:17 states: "He was afraid. . . ."

What had seemed, the night before, to be an inconsequential rest stop—the only reason he stops there is because the sun goes down; there's nothing special about this place—he now understands to be "awesome . . . none other than the house of God" (Genesis 28:17).

This is what's so important for us to see: experiencing God in this place was certainly not what Jacob expected. He's surprised. But he really shouldn't be, because God is not somewhere else. God is always right here.

The reality that God is not somewhere else is perhaps even more powerfully communicated through biblical poetry such as Psalm 139, in which David prays: "Where can I go from your Spirit? Where can I flee from your presence? If I go up to the heavens, you are there; if I make my bed in the depths, you are there. If I rise on the wings of the dawn, if I settle on the far side of the sea, even there your hand will guide me, your right hand will hold me fast" (Psalm 139:7–10).

David is reflecting on the joyous wonder of God being everywhere. That's a message we often celebrate. We love the accessibility of "everywhere." It leaves all the options open. We want that accessibility. We get panicky when our accessibility feels limited. Perhaps the most desperate spiritual question I've been asked at our church is not, "What's God's will for my life" but "What's the WiFi password?"!

We love the idea that God is everywhere. We can access God anywhere: at church, at home, at the beach, in the mountains. . . . Isn't that so convenient? But there's a potentially less convenient side of that coin. It's the sometimes less-than-joyous reality that God is not elsewhere. In other words, if God is to be "found" he is to be found right where you are.

If God is everywhere, as the Bible clearly reveals, then the less convenient truth is that God is also here. And if God is here then perhaps I should stay.

God in the Place

A quick word about place.

It's important to realize that the reason to stay is not the place, ultimately. Places change. The reason to stay in a place is that God is in the place. There may be good reason to leave a place, but "God is not here" is not one of them. God is not somewhere else.

God's presence extends to the place, and so God can be known there. The place—specific places—can become incredibly important to us personally (as I'll discuss later), but the real value of a place is that it serves as a specific context or container in and through which God makes himself known.

Jacob built an altar on the side of the road where he crashed for the night, not because the place itself was special, but because he experienced God there. The place served as a container for the presence of God.

The essential truth is that God is always here. But it's almost impossible to really know that if we're always moving to new places. If we're always moving and our context is perpetually changing, then there's little we can point to as a physical example of the stability of God. I need physical examples of that truth. I've learned that we need to "stay in a place long enough to begin to unpack the reality" of the God who is always there, who is stable and does not change, and to whom we always can return because he hasn't moved.[20]

My first clear memories of a place are of Woodman Lane: a three-acre patch of ground in the Northern California foothills which became our home when I was four. We built a house, barns, and fences. We planted trees and raised pigs, sheep, and chickens. We worked and played there. It's where I grew up. It's the house I left when I went to college, and it's the only home to which I've ever returned. It's the reference point for my childhood. After more than forty years, my folks still live there. It's still the gathering place for our family. It's still home. The trees cast deeper shadows in the afternoon and the old barns have faded and sagged. Grandkids now rediscover hidden wonders by the creek. But the place is still there, serving as a tangible expression of stability that helps me believe the truth about God.

Now let's add the beautiful relational concept of "with" to the tangible presence of "place."

The nature of the relationship into which you and I are invited by God is sometimes referred to as the covenant (or the promise). God's "Covenant" with Israel—the big promise reiterated several times throughout the Old Testament Scriptures and then realized with unprecedented tangibility in the Incarnation—is that God is with us. "I will be your God and you will be my people" says the LORD.[21] And the notion that God is with people makes all the difference in the world. For instance, when Moses charges Joshua to lead the Hebrew community into Jericho, he says, "Be strong and courageous. Do not be afraid; do not be discouraged; for the LORD your God is with you wherever you go" (Joshua 1:9). Here's another example: In David's testimony about his darkest days he declares, "Even though I walk through the darkest valley, I will fear no evil, for you are with me" (Psalm 23:4).

In fact, hundreds of times in Scripture we're told, "Do not fear," and the single reason we're given time and time again is simply this: God is with us.

Here's one more example. Being "with" is such a core character trait of God that in telling the story of the birth of the Messiah, Matthew recalls Isaiah's prophecy, "The virgin will conceive and give birth to a son, and they will call him Immanuel"—which means "God with us" (Matthew 1:23; see Isaiah 8:8 and 10).

In other words, God is with us in this place. We can experience God at home or at work, at school or at church, in Wisconsin or California. God is here. God is not elsewhere. It is both God's nature (omnipresence) and God's character (faithfulness) that call us to root our security in the stability of God. "The LORD is my rock and my fortress," declares King David (Psalm 18:2). The rock-solid reliability of God means we can experience God wherever we are.

God is not elsewhere. Wherever I go, God's already there. Wherever I am, God is.

But Doesn't God Call Us to Go?

What about God's calling Abram to "Go from your country, your people and your father's household and go to the land I will show you" (Genesis 12:1) or Christ's commissioning his disciples to "go and make disciples of all nations" (Matthew 28:19)? What about all the missionary journeys in Acts or the pilgrimage language in the Psalms? If God is here, with us, what about all the going? Isn't there a pretty strong biblical theme of people on the move?

Yes. But. Our restless culture says, "Go find what you're looking for." The Bible says, "Go because you've found what you're looking for." In other words, it is precisely God's faithful presence—God's stability—that enables people, or compels people, to go wherever God directs them. In both cases there is movement. But the movement that matters—that heals rather than hurts—is the movement motivated by having experienced God, not the wandering around in search of him.

Here are a few examples:

One of the earliest movements in Genesis is in chapter 12 when Abram moves away from his home and family in Ur. Echoing the Biblical language, we refer to Abram's "leaving" Ur, but, in fact, he is sent by God for a specific purpose.[22] Therefore, Abram's movement matters.

Consider, by contrast, an early scene in Moses's life in which he leaves Egypt. He flees following his own impassioned reaction to witnessing violent injustice (Exodus 2:11–14). And for the next forty years Moses lives in relative obscurity; only God sees the value of these decades. We'd likely never hear of Moses again if it weren't for his second big move: a return to Egypt (Exodus 4:18–31). The difference between the two trips? In the first he's escaping. In the second he's being sent. It's critical to see that Moses doesn't go to Egypt in search of God. He goes to Egypt as a direct result of having experienced God right where he was. And clearly, Moses's return to Egypt is movement that matters.

There is no example in the Bible of a person who leaves in search of God and finds him.[23] But there are several examples of people who encounter God right where they are and are consequently sent. It is precisely the experience of becoming aware of God's presence here that births the faith that he will also be there—the place to which he is sending us. The confidence to move to another place is rooted in our experience with God in this place.

Meaningful movement is dependent upon such confidence. What does Christ say directly following his most famous command to move? After commissioning his disciples to "go and make disciples of all nations," Jesus assures them, reminding them of the truth they've learned through experience, "surely I am with you always" (Matthew 28:20).

While the life of faith often influences a variety of practical questions that could more or less fit in a category titled "should we stay or should we go?," there's an important sense in which it doesn't matter. It's possible to have a wandering heart while your body stays put. Conversely, it's possible to remain spiritually grounded while going to a new place. The real issue is deeper than staying or going. The real issue is that deep in our hearts, at our core, we all carry the curse of Cain (Genesis 4:10–12). We are all restless wanderers trying to find our way home. And so many voices are calling our name, demanding our devotion, promising the fulfillment that only One can truly provide. My hope is that amidst all of our searching for a peaceful and meaningful life we will recognize that we were created to root our lives in Christ. We can and we must find what we're looking for in him. As famous restless wanderer, St. Augustine, finally confessed, "Our hearts are restless until we find our rest in Thee."

First, Stay

When St. Benedict organized his monasteries in sixth-century Italy, as the Roman Empire crumbled around him, he welcomed anyone who would come. But what he required, in order for anyone to join the monastery, was that the person make three vows.

First was the vow of stability. Benedict required a monk to promise to seek God in this place with this community under the guidelines established by this Rule. Didn't Benedict believe that God is everywhere? Of course he did. But he also knew that if you couldn't learn to find God here, it's very unlikely that you'd learn to experience him anywhere else.

In his book *Lovers of the Place*, the late Trappist monk Francis Kline uses the compelling phrase, "a particular monastic church" to refer to a faith community which "through the pascal mystery . . . now present in the worshiping community, becomes part of the heavenly liturgy."[24] This got me to thinking . . . could my modern church be my monastery? Could my submission to worshiping in this way, with these people, in this place, be, for me, a step into the historic monastic experience?

How can I participate in the "heavenly liturgy?" How can I join, with all creation of all time, in the rejoicing of heaven if not through the specific, localized, here-and-now reality of my local church? In the church, I access the eternal through the temporal. I taste the endless expanse of heaven in the local. The doorway into the throne room of heaven is, for me, located at 561 Lincoln Boulevard.

When I begin with the truth that God is not somewhere else, I can embrace my local church as the particular access point to the timeless, limitless reality of heaven. I can love the local church as essential, rather than consuming the local church as optional. When this truth is carried into a broader, social perspective, the church becomes a valued treasure, not a necessary evil. I can see the local church as flawed and broken, as another failed attempt at institutionalizing spirituality. Or I can see the local church as a glimmer of light reflecting something of the wonder and beauty and power of the Kingdom of the One True God.

Two Practices

In order for you to grow, authentically and practically, into experiencing the omnipresence of God, I'd encourage two practices.

First, consider the words you use when you pray. Specifically, stop asking God to be with you. It can be easy to reinforce harmful or even false theology with the words we use. A phrase I often hear spoken in prayer is the simple request for God to "be with me." Often, when we don't have a more specific need, we'll pray, "Lord, please be with me today." Now, to be clear, there's nothing wrong with asking God to be with you or to be with your mother, your kids, etc. In fact, even Moses, when faced with a seemingly impossible challenge, once prayed something very similar, saying to God, "If your Presence does not go with us, do not send us up from here" (Exodus 33:15). Asking God to be with you is understandable and is certainly not bad. It's just unnecessary.

God is already with you. God is already there. My concern is that praying, "God, be with me at school today," gently but firmly reinforces the perception that he's not. You may not feel God at school but to say that God's not there blatantly contradicts Scripture.

A better prayer is, "God, help me to be with you at school today." That is to say, "Enable me to remain faithful to you, to be aware of your presence, to follow you. . . ." God's stability is the constant. He is always there, always here, always with. We can count on that and not doubt it. We should pray instead that he would help us to be with him.

Second, reconsider your view of corporate worship and the ways you talk and invite others into it. Start approaching corporate worship as a rhythm rather than as an event.

Experiencing God is undermined by the all-too-common assumption that life with God is essentially a series of spiritual events, like concerts or conferences. And in order to experience a meaningful spiritual life you need to find the right event. You need to go there. It's the spiritual version of the experience economy. You need that experience happening at that place at that time (and you'll want to take a selfie to prove you were there).

Increasingly, at least in American evangelical culture, "church" is seen as an event. Worship gatherings are designed, promoted, and executed like live shows, meant to "service" the audience. Church-as-event or viewing church as an event to attend rather than a rhythm to practice contributes to an even larger misunderstanding of spirituality-as-event. Events are either on or off, they're either happening now, or they're not. If I carry this church-as-event view into my greater understanding of relationship with God, I will develop a spirituality that is insufficient, largely irrelevant, and inconsistently applied to real life.

I'd urge you instead to reorient your view of worship as rhythm: as a practice you repeat, often, with the long term in mind, as a way of life, as a way of participating in the created order, and in all eternity. Rhythms shape us. Regular practices form us. Events may entertain, but routines change lives. Rhythms carry a potency that events can only dream about.

Worship-as-event thinking is the culprit behind the common and growing trend of sampling Sunday church gatherings like ice cream flavors. The insidious truth is that the church, herself, has perpetuated this approach with cheap incentives for attendance and language that leverages a fear of "missing what God is doing." We need to return to an ancient approach to worship as rhythm. We should be called to worship by the rising and setting of the sun, not some here today, gone tomorrow attraction. We should gather with our community around Word and Sacrament because it's the Sabbath, because this is what we do, because this is our practice, our routine, our constant norm—because of "place" and "with."

Walking to the Monastery in the Mountains

In these short selections at the end of each chapter, I offer some of my experiences learning the lessons of this book.

After an absolutely wonderful month-long sabbatical with my family in Italy, I say goodbye to my wife and three kids. They navigate the security lines at the Fiumicino Airport: the start of a long flight home to California. One final time, they turn and wave. I am jarred by the sudden and intense reality that I am alone.

Now I'm off to encounter whatever it is God has for me in these next three weeks—walking the Cammino di San Benedetto and then "monk camp"—as the kids are calling it. Guide my steps, Good Shepherd. Speak, for your servant is listening. May the words of my mouth and the meditations of my heart be acceptable in your sight, O Lord, my Rock, my Redeemer.

I walk today. The bus I planned to take from Carsoli to my starting point on the Cammino di San Benedetto in Castel di Tora never arrived. So, after waiting too long, I realize I should just start walking. Which I do, sixteen miles, on busy roads, uphill to Orvinio.

I'm not sure what the purpose of today's walk was, except, perhaps, to break me loose of my plan, to feel out of control and to have to surrender to that.

Today is another fifteen miles of steep climbing, now along the actual Cammino route. I visit the caves where Benedict is believed to have spent some time, and where he was, according to tradition, given poisoned wine by monks. These were the men who first asked him to be their abbot, but then rebelled due to Benedict's highly disciplined devotion. According to the story told by Pope Gregory the Great, when Benedict made the sign of the cross over the chalice it exploded.

It is amazing to imagine monks living in these caves. Some are quite large—as big as living rooms—and others are only big enough to sleep in. All are in the cliffs high above the clear blue waters of the Aniene River.

The cave in which St. Benedict was given the wine has been made into a rustic chapel. Graffiti, including names and dates, some as old as 1939, were scratched over the frescos.

After a challenging ten-plus hours of hiking, I reach Subiaco, the ancient Benedictine monastery built high into the cliffs above the ruins of Nero's summer residence. I plan to spend tomorrow exploring this remarkable site, so I press on to tackle the final two miles farther above the historic monastery to a small convent and retreat house called Casa di Preghiera (House of Prayer) San Biagio, run by Salesian sisters.

I'm startled when a nun in a tiny car pulls over and motions for me to get in. I'm so spent that I instantly comply, shocking myself with my own willingness to accept the ride. I spend the next several moments struggling to communicate my destination. She is speaking rapidly in Italian. We are completely failing to communicate as she shifts gears and climbs higher and higher up the mountain. Finally, she pats my knee and says, "Rest."

We arrive at the convent. I realize the nun is Sister M.L., the Superior. She was notified by the place I had stayed the previous night to be on the lookout for an American pilgrim. The view from this place is unparalleled. Perched high above the monastery in Subiaco, it was built on the site of the hermitage of Romanus, the monk who, for two years, lowered food in a basket at the end of a long rope to the young hermit, Benedict.

The next day, I explore Subiaco—Benedict's monastery built deep into caves in the cliffs above the headwaters of the Aniene. I am alone for hours in this series of rock rooms. All the walls and ceilings are covered in beautiful paintings depicting scenes from Benedict's life as told in Pope Gregory's account of his life.

I have entered another world.

Powerfully complementing the force of this rich, ancient site is the hospitality of the sisters at the House of Prayer. Mealtimes here are joy-filled feasts. There are several guests at the house, but I am the only American and the only non-Catholic. This, plus the fact that I am here studying St. Benedict and on my way to the monastery in Norcia, Benedict's birthplace, makes for wonderful conversation. I'm grateful especially for Fr. M., an African priest, who translates our conversations with an enormous smile and even larger laughter.

After dinner, I'm informed that Sr. M.P.G., the ninety-five-year-old co-founder of the convent, wants to see me. It is made clear that this is an exceptional invitation. I rise to walk toward the private dining room where Sister takes her meals but turn to find her standing at the doorway, her tiny body supported by Sr. M.L.

She looks at me intently and speaks powerful, specific, deeply encouraging words (in Italian—Fr. M. translated) over my life and ministry. Then she says, "We serve the same Jesus, the same Lord, we preach the same gospel. Let's work for the unity of Christ's church. . . ."

Deeply moved, I ask if she will pray for me. She says, "Yes, but would you first give me a blessing?" I make the sign on the cross on her forehead and pray for her. Then she blesses me and prays. Fr. M. is still translating but I'm not hearing the words. I am so deep in prayer. She lowers her hand from my forehead to my face, where, tenderly cupping my cheeks in her hands, she continues to pray.

The following day, at the Benedictine monastery of Norcia, my mind is flooded, there is so much to take in.

After traveling by train, by foot, and by bus, I arrive in the early afternoon. It has rained hard all morning, but, thankfully, the skies have cleared. I wait for a while, hoping I've chosen the correct place to exit the bus. I'm just outside the old walled portion of the town. Finally, a small car pulls up and a monk—young, shaved head, long red beard, wearing a thick blue "work" habit—climbs out. I wave and begin moving in his direction.

Brother A. introduces himself while navigating the tight turns of the tiny roads that lead us up the mountain.

I feel as if I am living a scene from a movie and keep reminding myself that "this is actually happening." A year earlier, I could never have imagined this moment. Four days ago I waved goodbye to my family as they returned to the States, then I walked in near-total solitude along a portion of the Cammino di San Benedetto, and now I am in a car with a bearded Benedictine monk careening through the birthplace of St. Benedict.

When we arrive, Brother A. shows me to the refectory, where a place is already set for me at the guest's table. My name is printed on the napkin ring. "You want a beer?" he asks, with a grin and a twinkle in his eye.

I am shown the daily schedule and invited to participate in nearly everything. The next prayer time is Compline, and it starts in fifteen minutes. Brother A. encourages me to participate. "It's part of the experience," he says. But then he reconsiders and suggests sleeping in the first day . . . which means not joining the monks for the dark hours of prayer and waiting until 6 a.m. to join them in the church.

CHAPTER 2
Stability and Self
The Need to Not Run

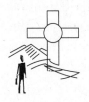

"Where I am,
my servant also will be."

—JESUS, JOHN 12:26

Run!
Every great movie has a chase scene. Think through your favorite film . . . can you identify some kind of pursuit? Is it a car chase on a multi-lane freeway? An around-the-globe tracking of a rogue agent? A sprint through stalled traffic to reach the church before she marries the wrong guy? It seems every good story involves someone who's running.

Why do you think chase scenes are so common? Is it just that they're exciting? Or do they resonate with some deeper reality in the human experience?

You might summarize the Bible as the story of a good God's loving pursuit of humanity. What is God doing in the story? God is pursuing. And what is humanity doing? We're running. Maybe it's fear, maybe it's pride, maybe it's ignorance, but it seems our tendency is to respond to God's offer of companionship and salvation by running away.

Many of us could tell the story of when we finally stopped running from God and repented, or turned around, and started to run toward him. These are our stories of surrender. And though that major conflict is now settled for many of us, there are still days when we sense in ourselves the tendency to respond to God's offer for closer intimacy with him by running away. Maybe you've recognized the tendency in yourself to respond to God's offer for a new level of trust by pulling back . . . by running.

This is why stability is so important for us. Embracing stability is how we stop running and allow ourselves to be found.[25]

The logic is simple: if God is here then I must not run away. I need to stay. If God is here I need to be here, too. Embracing stability is the opposite of restless wandering. It's how I will come to know the God who is always here.

If "stability" is not a word you've often used as a personal value, I imagine you've discussed the power of perseverance. I bet you've nodded your head in admiration of a friend's steadfast commitment through a challenging season. It's easy to encourage our kids to "stick with it" or to "stay put" until the job is done. These words and phrases reveal an almost inherent recognition of the spiritual value of stability.

Externally, stability fortifies the health of a community— both the people and the place. Stable communities seem to engender more stability. But long before its impact is ever felt by others, the critical seed of a personal commitment to stability grows beneath the surface. This commitment to resist the temptation to run eventually matures into a tree that shelters others.

We're talking about real inner peace. We're talking about a quality of stillness inside, a settled-ness of the soul. And it's not just a peace that makes us feel good. It's a peace that enables us to stand against the storms of this life. We don't have to run around anxiously when trouble looms, because God is here, and our home is in him. This conviction frees us from a life of striving for or running away. Our patient perseverance expresses a "contented residency in God."[26]

In her excellent commentary on the Rule of St. Benedict, Joan Chittister writes, "Life is not easy and life is not to be lived as if it were, for fear that when we really need internal fortitude we will not have developed it. It is an important insight for all of us. We must develop the rigor it takes to live through what life deals us. We can't set out to get holy in the hope that we will then automatically become faithful. We must require fidelity of ourselves even when we fail, in the hope that someday, as a result, we will finally become holy."[27]

Think of a several-hundred-year-old oak tree planted by a river, roots going deep, branches reaching wide. It's solid. "Stripped of our anxious transience," we, too, can be planted like a tree beside water.[28]

We're not talking simply about staying at the same address (though that might help, and we'll discuss that in later chapters). We're really talking about an inner quality of strength that keeps us from running away, that keeps us from constantly trying to escape the truth, that positions us to become a source of stability for others.

Ancient Solutions for Modern Ills

What instantly captivated me about St. Benedict was that he understood and named the core hindrance to true spiritual transformation: the spirit of the gyrovague—the impulse to leave, to respond by running.

The first few paragraphs of Benedict's *Rule* are a remarkably insightful description of the all-too-common trend of people moving from church to church, receiving hospitality but moving on before anything is required of them. When I first discovered it, I felt Benedict was describing my core frustration with the church in twenty-first-century American Christianity. I was then surprised when I turned back to the introduction and learned that the *Rule* was first published in the sixth century—1,400 years ago. I remember thinking, *If this guy understands my problem so well, maybe he could help me find a good solution.*

Benedict believed that in order to experience God one needs to stay put. But he recognized how difficult this is for our restless hearts. So, he turned the value into a vow. Why is that important? Because a vow implies a struggle.

Maybe you've made a vow or two. If you're married you made a marriage vow, a statement that ultimately boils down to the promise to love and remain faithful to your spouse. If you're baptized you made a baptism vow (or your parents made it for you as a promise, and then you grew up to confirm that promise), the promise to follow Jesus for the rest of your life. If you're an ordained minister, you made a vow to the church. If you're a medical doctor, you took the Hippocratic Oath, which is its own kind of covenant. And so on.

Here's what's so intense and confrontational about vows: they imply struggle and difficulty. That's why we make vows: to fortify us for battles of the will!

Part of what a marriage vow reveals is some level of awareness of the challenge inherent in being married. The core part of a marriage ceremony is this public statement that acknowledges that the relationship you're entering into is going to be so difficult it's going to require a vow.

That's what vows do—they acknowledge right up front that this is going to be hard. There will be days when everything in me wants to bail out. So, in order to stick with this as I intend, I'm going to have to start by making a vow.

Benedict required those entering his monasteries to make three vows, the first of which was the vow of stability. The monk promised to live with these specific people in this specific place under this specific *Rule* for the rest of his life. Stability is the opposite of restlessness.

Benedict's vow of stability was "arguably the central concern of monastic life."[29] Benedict points to it early in the *Rule* when he refers to the monastery as a spiritual workshop where "stability in the community" is a necessary condition for spiritual growth. Later, in his short chapter on receiving monks into the monastery, he mentions it twice, first as a condition of continuing the year-long process of joining the monastery, and second as the initial part of the promise made in the presence of the entire community when a new monk is formally received into the monastery.[30] Benedict sees stability as the critical foundation on which "fidelity to monastic life and obedience" depend. As one monk said to me, plainly, "If you don't stay, you can't be a monk." It's stability that enables true, ongoing personal conversion that is so central to the monastic experience (and, I'm sure Benedict would agree, the Christian experience).

In Italy, I asked a young monk how the vow of stability had shaped his experience so far. I think I was expecting a response that had to do with the "for the rest of his life" aspect of the vow. What he said was refreshingly practical. "Sometimes stability is just being faithful to staying put for an hour of prayer. You simply bring that commitment to the struggle." You may feel like leaving, but you commit to stay, even one hour at a time.

We live in a world of great insecurity. But Benedict's world may have felt even less secure. Born a few generations after the sack of Rome, he grew up in a volatile world plagued by constant warfare and widespread social and political insecurity. In parts of society where we enjoy a sense of relative security, we're often plagued by the equally damaging malady of disintegration. Our lives are fragmented into many seemingly unrelated parts. There's work life, home life, family life, social life, spiritual life, "as if we have several separately compartmentalized existences."[31]

It's the insecurity and disintegration of our lives—the fear and the chaos—that makes us want to run. But it's not only from outside pressures that we are trying to escape. The strongest, most ferocious temptation to run is from within. It threatens to take control when a person can no longer face him/herself.

The Need to Not Run Away

In *Seeking God*, Esther de Waal argues that stability addresses the "very basic demand . . . the need not to run away."[32]

She writes, "Stability says there must be no evasion; instead attend to the real, to the real necessity however unconformable that might be. Stability brings us from a feeling of alienation, perhaps from the escape into fantasy and daydreaming, into the state of reality. It will not allow us to evade the inner truth of whatever it is that we have to do, however dreary and boring and apparently unfruitful that may seem."

She continues, "Stability is achieved through perseverance, through holding on even under great strain, without weakening or trying to escape."[33]

Exceptions? There are situations and conditions which clearly call for a person to run away. Those include abusive relationships, and toxic, destructive environments. I'm not saying we should stay no matter what. But I do want to challenge the idea that as soon as things get uncomfortable, we should leave. I do want to confront the notion that "this is hard" equals "I should leave." The need to not run away is an uncomfortable topic precisely because it reveals our points of personal pain—the very thing from which we want to run.

I clearly remember the intensity of the desire to run away into a fantasy or daydream during an especially painful season of my life. My four-year-old son was diagnosed with leukemia and endured years of hospital stays and the sometimes-barbaric reality of chemotherapy. His physical pain was often amplified by his lack of understanding. As a child he was not able to comprehend the long-term purposes of our efforts to treat the disease. From his perspective, we were constantly forcing him to do things he didn't want to do. The daily pills and weekly trips to the oncologist hurt. Our insisting that they would help was infuriating. The emotional toll taken on my wife and me during this season was unprecedented. Sometimes, on the rare quiet evening, we would attempt to abandon our reality for a couple of hours by watching a movie. And while losing ourselves in a story other than our own provided a kind of temporary escape, I remember the dreadful feeling that would forcefully re-enter my mind the moment I realized the movie was coming to a close. It was as if our brief foray into fantasy would only dam up the regular flow of pain, not avoid it. Once the daydream was over the dam would release and the dread of real life would rush in with renewed vengeance. We would experience the initial feelings of shock and sadness all over again as our emotions, which had been momentarily manipulated by another's story, crashed back to the reality of our story with concussive force.

Because I was in pain, I wanted to escape. But escaping wasn't the answer. We had to learn how to live in the pain.

To borrow de Waal's language, our situation's very basic demand was the need not to run away. Any so-called solution which required a separation of our real life into fabricated parts was both unrealistic and completely impotent. Disintegrating cancer from the rest of our life was impossible. We desperately needed deep inner healing but not independent from our real world.

What good would that do? How would any advice or counsel that failed to consider the whole of our lives help us?

This is why stability is the necessary foundation for true spiritual growth: it requires a level of honesty about life which we simply cannot experience if our response to pain, disappointment, or difficulty is to leave. Stability confronts that primal urge to escape. It bars the door. It says, "You're going to have to deal with this pain. It cannot be avoided. Now turn around and face it."

Step into It

When I was in high school, I played football and baseball. Though I was a hard hitter in football, I was a below-average hitter in baseball. But I won a starting spot as catcher (probably because that was the position in baseball most like football).

These were the good old days when baserunners were taught to run through the catcher if there was a close play at the plate. The strategy, for the baserunner, was to hit the catcher so hard that he would drop the ball, allowing the runner to score.

In these situations, the advantage is always the runner's. (Do a quick search for "collisions at the plate" on YouTube if you have no idea what I'm talking about.) The reason is simple: momentum. The runner has ninety feet of momentum while the catcher is literally standing still, waiting for the ball.

But here's what I learned and learned to love. By facing and stepping into the runner, I could alter the physics. By grounding myself, facing the runner, and not just anticipating the hit, but initiating it, I could change the game. I could make it more like football. And even if I got knocked down it was a win if I could just hold on to the ball. Runner's out.

I went back and forth about whether to tell this story but here's why I share it (I know it probably sounds like an attempt to relive the glory days . . . and I guess it is . . .). But here's the truth: I need images like this in my life today. Because all day long it feels like I'm facing collisions at the plate, such as when I see the caller ID and I know the criticism that's coming . . . and I'm caught off guard, but they've got ninety feet of momentum.

What do I want to do? Send to voicemail. Avoid. What do I need to do? Deal with it. Face it. I need to not run.

I need images like this in my life today when I see so many in my community in pain . . . when they get hit with the diagnosis or the divorce papers or the deep disappointment and I know that the next season of their life is going to be really hard. I need images like this in my life when I see pain coming and my heart screams, "Run!" But my head knows that you can't avoid real life; you must face it.

You may get knocked on your butt. But the hope is that maybe, ultimately, when the dust settles and the screaming is silenced, you will have held on. The hope is you won't avoid it, you won't pretend the brokenness isn't happening, you won't try to ignore it and hope it goes away.

Having a sick child was a class of pain that was difficult to ignore. More common are the subtle faults and fears. We've become quite sophisticated in our efforts to avoid these less obvious, but similarly destructive demons. Non-stop activity, too many relationships, even good things like family, food, and work can be twisted to mask the brokenness inside caused by selfishness and sin. Stability is just as important when wrestling these less obvious obstacles to peace as it is when facing overwhelming fear or sorrow. When tempted to pretend and avoid, we should be honest and we should stay. Stability is the critical foundation that enables real growth and ongoing conversion.

This is how we'll experience a spirituality that makes a difference in real life.

A Little Strictness

In our culture, you can have anything you want anytime you want it. At least that's what you've been told and so that's likely what you believe. And in those few times when you actually get what you want when you want it the tendency is to believe you deserve it. You give yourself the credit. This is the way life's supposed to be! The rest of the time, when you don't get what you want when you want it you fashion yourself the victim. It's not your fault. If only . . .

Confronting this hyper-consumeristic perspective on reality are these remarkable words from St. Benedict, who teaches his followers to "embrace a little strictness" for "the good of all concerned."[34] This is the (perhaps astonishing) notion that one would choose to limit one's choices for a greater purpose . . . that the good one "gets" from limiting consumption is ultimately more valuable than anything one could consume.

Instead of perpetually moving on to the next you might choose to stay. Rather than ceaselessly pursuing more you might decide that's enough.

"Embrac[ing] a little strictness" is just a simple, practical discipline that we might apply to food or sleep or sex or any other good thing. But it's a powerful step into a way of living characterized by peaceful stability rather than the stupor of consumerism or the terror of chaos.

In *The Cloister Walk*, Kathleen Norris tells a story about preparing an omelet in the kitchen of her apartment in the Ecumenical Institute. When one of the brothers walked in, she offered, "How would you like your eggs?" The question stopped him. He looked confused. His dumbfounded expression caused her to realize the obvious: "He's a monk, which means no one ever asks him how he likes his eggs."

She writes, "To eat in a monastery refectory is an exercise in humility; daily, one is reminded to put communal necessity before individual preference. While consumer culture speaks only to preferences, treating even whims as needs to be granted (and the sooner the better), monastics sense that this pandering to delusions of self-importance weakens the true self, and diminishes our ability to distinguish desires from needs. It's a price they're not willing to pay."[35]

There's power in embracing a perspective on life in which personal preferences are not valued, or in some cases, even acknowledged.

The Apostle Paul makes an astounding statement at the end of his letter to the Christians in Philippi. He writes, "I have learned to be content whatever the circumstances." How many people do you run into throughout the day whose joy and peace are unaffected by their circumstances? Most seem to be almost entirely ruled by them! Paul continues, "I have learned the secret of being content in any and every situation, whether well fed or hungry, whether living in plenty or in want."

What's the secret?! Paul declares it, "I can do all this through him who gives me strength" (Philippians 4:11–13).

So, here are my questions: How did Paul learn that? How did he develop the ability to experience true peace in the midst of chaos? Or pain? Or criticism?

The answer? He stayed. He didn't run. He pressed in. He faced adversity of all kinds. We commonly think of Paul as always on the move. He's famous for his many journeys, for traveling and preaching in far off places. His letters commonly include plans to go somewhere else or return to where he's been for a brief visit. But a closer look reveals a remarkable level of perseverance. "I press on toward the goal," he writes the Philippians (3:14).

He repeatedly mentions his enduring physical suffering rather than abandoning his mission, pointing to his own scars as evidence of his commitment. He reminds the Galatians, "I bear on my body the marks of Jesus" (6:17). He charges the Colossians, "Remember my chains" (4:18). He shares with the Corinthian church an intimate glimpse into a personal struggle—he calls it "a thorn in my flesh"—from which he pleads three times for relief. He writes, "But [the Lord] said to me, 'My grace is sufficient for you, for my power is made perfect in weakness'" (2 Corinthians 12:8–9). In other words (if you'll allow a loose paraphrase): "With my power you can learn how to live with this, Paul! Your body wants to avoid the pain, but I want to teach you something that can only be learned while you're in it: My powerful presence is right here."

Paul learns this lesson through stability even in suffering. Yes, at first glance, we see Paul always on the move, but the inner man is unshakable. He stands firm. That's how he learns the secret of constant contentment. He practices deep inner personal stability, come what may. "Finally," he instructs the Ephesians, "be strong in the Lord . . . so . . . you may be able to stand your ground, and after you have done everything, to stand" (6:10, 13).

The real goal is not staying at one address. The real goal is stability of the heart.

Stability of the Heart

In *Seeking God*, Esther de Waal quotes Metropolitan Anthony Bloom, who explains: "The fact of being limited by a line drawn on the ground" does not in itself make one stable. Instead, "we discovered that at the heart of stability there is the certitude that God is everywhere, that we have no need to seek God elsewhere, that if I can't find God here I shan't find Him anywhere, because the kingdom of God begins within us. Consequently the first thing about stability is the certitude that I stand before God wholly, immobile so to speak – the place hardly matters."[36]

"This," concludes de Waal, "is the stability of the heart."[37]

Practice Being Here

We are only here, now. The past is gone. We can't get back to it. The future is not yet here. We cannot yet experience it. We can only always be here, now.

And so we must. Here's why: not just because here, now, is the only place we can be. But also (and more importantly) here, now, is the only place we can experience God.

Because God created time, God exists outside of its limits. God is fully present to all time—past, present, future—at the same time, at this present moment. God is fully present to the past. But we cannot be. The past is locked to us. God is fully present to the future. But we aren't there yet. The future is beyond our reach.

The only time we can ever experience God is now. The only place we can ever experience God is here: right where we are. And so all we need—both to heal from the past and to prepare for the future—can only ever be received from God here, now, in this present moment.

It's simply crucial that we learn how to be present.

Three Ways to Practice Being Here

Here are some ways I've practiced being present to the moment that I've found very helpful. Perhaps one of these will work well for you.

1) *Brewing tea.*

During a season of intense grief, I was given a loose-leaf tea steeper. It became a powerful tool of healing. Brewing tea takes just a few minutes, which is a perfect amount of time to start practicing being present. When being present to the moment feels nearly impossible, I will practice paying attention to right here, right now, for the one to three minutes it takes for my tea to steep (less time for green tea; more time for black). Pouring hot water into the clear steeper, I pay attention to the darkening of the water as the heat pulls the flavor from the leaves. I pay attention to the change and to the stillness. If I'm able to continue for another moment, I pour the tea into a cup and hold it with two hands close enough to my face to feel the heat and smell the fragrance. I close my eyes and breathe in the steam. I feel. Closing my eyes intensifies the sensitivity of my other senses: touch, smell, and then taste. I'll draw in the first sip and feel the warmth fill my body. Gratitude comes easily in this moment. And if I'm able to continue, I'll enjoy the whole cup, raising it gently with both hands, sipping it slowly. I've given myself permission to just be here, now, while I drink this tea.

2) *Taking pictures.*

I began taking pictures in a season when I knew I needed to slow down. I practiced paying attention to whatever was right in front of me: my toddler's dimpled hands, tender bright green tips of pine, patterns in tractor wheels, sunsets. The anticipation of seeing something wonderful helped me pay attention and stay in the present. The part in me that needs to constantly achieve was satisfied with the simple accomplishment of capturing an image. Neither the quality nor the use of the picture was the point. Being here, now, and pausing just long enough to capture something of that moment—that's what helped me learn how to be. At other times in life, taking pictures can do the very opposite—it can pull you out of the moment. Instead of experiencing the magic of Christmas morning with your kids as a participant, you step out of the moment and distance yourself as an observer with a camera. This can pull you out of the game and turn you into just another photographer on the sidelines. And the now-common instinct to immediately post/share the image with unseen others online only makes it worse. Be careful with this one. But if you're drowning in regret or grief from the past or if you're wild with fear about the future, try going for a walk with your camera and capturing images of this present moment.

3) Journaling.

I began journaling daily in a time of confusion. I didn't know what was true and just needed get stuff down on paper. This proved helpful, and so I continue to this day. I begin by writing the date, the place, the time. September 20. Kitchen table. 5:51 a.m. Less important from a record-keeping perspective, is the practice of "getting here now" that I find helpful. Next, I make note of something about that moment. Like, "The house is dark and silent." Or, "Feeling tired." Or, "Reading Psalm 19." This helps gather the scattered forces of my soul. Different from the explorer's detailed documenting or the pre-teen's emotional outpouring/processing, my purpose is contemplation. It's a pen and paper kind of praying. It's a way to be attentive and to (literally) take note of what's going on in and all around me.

One of the most well-known theologians in the ancient church is a man named Augustine. He was a fourth-century African who was also a citizen of Rome. His sermons and philosophical writings are viewed as really significant by early Christians from both the East and the West. He's considered a "doctor" of the church. He's also famous for his rebellious youth. He was notorious for getting into trouble and living recklessly, and he fathered a child when he was a teenager. Later in his life, he wrote a book called *Confessions*. It's the book that contains this famous line: "You have made us for yourself, God, and our hearts are restless until they rest in you."

Augustine's story is that he looked for adventure, meaning, love, and peace in all sorts of places, but he always ended in destruction and disappointment—until he surrendered his heart to his creator and finally found, in God, the fulfillment he'd long searched for.

First Week at the Monastery

It feels disorienting to be a guest where the schedule is so strictly observed but no one is talking or giving instructions. It's "figure it out as you go." Graciously, Brother An. motioned for me to come into the dining room after Lauds (6 a.m. prayer) and offered me coffee. "We have the instant stuff," he whispered. When he noticed my hesitation as I scanned the table for cups, he instructed me to use a bowl.

There's a thick fog covering and filling the valley below the monastery. Birds are singing but I can't see any of them because of the fog. . . . I've stayed in monasteries that feel like retreat centers. . . . San Benedetto—at least a few hours in—definitely feels like a "workshop."

"Before lunch, since you're a first-time guest, the superior will wash your hands," informed Br. B.

My confused look must have prompted him to add, "I'm just letting you know since it might seem a little strange."

Before we sat for lunch, I was invited with a nod to approach the washbasin in the middle of the room. Father Prior poured warm water over my hands, looked me in the eye, and said, "Welcome."

Both nights here I've had very intense spiritual dreams . . . where the line between dream and reality is tough to discern. . . .

I rise, brush my teeth, and join the community in the chapel at 3 a.m. for Vigils. After an hour of chanting psalms, we move to an hour of personal reading.

I'm feeling overwhelmed by the thought of being here for two more weeks. I'm feeling tempted by the thought that this is a waste of time. I'm so tired. I'm praying that this experience will accomplish something good in me, in my family, and in our community.

The antiphons for Prime (9 a.m. prayer):

"Thou hast no need of my goods. Preserve me, O Lord, for I have put my trust in Thee."

Later in the day I get a chance to talk with Br. B. He shares small glimpses into his story which captivate me. We discuss the vow of stability, his plans to be a parish priest, his time in seminary, and his disappointments about the general focus on self that he has encountered in both the Church and the culture. He feels the monastery is the place where a person can join others in making a strong commitment to a life of devotion. "There's really only any value in what you do if it's offered to God," he says. The big test of faith was not joining the monastery, but "surrendering [his] desire to save souls." He shares, "I wanted to save souls . . . thousands of souls. I had to surrender that to God. I don't have a lot of contact with people [as a monk]."

I'm invited to accompany Br. A. to the small metal storage container "shop" to sell the beer. *Birra Nursia,* which the monks brew and bottle within the walls of the old city, is the monastery's primary method of self-sustenance. Our long talk is only momentarily interrupted by patrons, including, to my delight, uniformed police who make a generous purchase which they store in the trunk of their patrol car.

While I am filled with admiration and respect for Br. A.—his devotion to God is total, his passion for the Church unbending, and his willingness to share so genuinely with a guest like me is such a powerful example of the love of Christ—I return a bit discouraged. Clearly, Benedict envisioned the monastery as stability's context, not the fractured, come-and-go-as-you-please, drenched-in-consumerism North American church. Br. A. felt a better context for embracing stability for the non-monk would be the family.

Once again Br. B. is waiting for me at the chapel door as I enter at 3:30 a.m. I can barely see straight. He is alert and focused. He hands me the prayer book with several places marked with ribbons and adds, "Today is the Feast of the Nativity of John the Baptist, so we'll mostly be using this book." Then he hands me a second volume. It has no English translation. I give up trying to follow along with the Latin within a few minutes. Instead, I read Matthew's and Luke's accounts of John's life.

I expected this to be a peaceful place, and in several significant ways it is. But so far, it's mostly felt very challenging to me. I'm not sure why yet. I think part of it is feeling out of place. Part of it is feeling tired or hungry or both. Mostly I feel lonely. I should lean into that loneliness and receive Christ there . . . in the loneliness.

Later, I wrestle with how busy the day feels because it is broken into so many small pieces: two meals and seven times of prayer. I reflect on feeling more productive when I skip the afternoon prayer time in order to write for a longer period of time. Part of my problem, though, is that I have such an entrenched need for productivity, and praying doesn't feel very productive.

CHAPTER 3
Stability and Relationships
Monks Helped My Marriage

"The essence of anxiety is not being able to stay put.
By simply standing still, I face calmly the unknown
. . . but in order to do that I need strength. And this
strength is possessed by an individual only so long as he
doesn't separate his lot from that of the others.
He can't lose sight of the essential thing, that he is an
intimate part of a community."[38]

—MILENA JESENSKÁ

Recently my wife and I attended an event. Shortly after we arrived, a woman we know, who had a small part in what was happening that night, saw us and made her way toward us with a big smile and a surprised-to-see-you look on her face.

"Why are you here?" she asked us, the way you do when you don't know that one part of your life is somehow connected to another part of your life. "We're here for you," we said.

"You're here for me?!" she exclaimed, repeating the phrase, soaking it in, basking in the value of the statement, its significance, and all that it represented to her in that moment. We are here for you.

The Critical Role of Community

Benedict's primary purpose for writing the *Rule* was to provide a guide for personal transformation. Speaking directly to the reader, he began, "Listen, my son. . . ."[39] But it's equally clear that the context he envisions for personal transformation is a committed community. In other words, Benedict's *Rule* provides some brilliant guidance for soul formation, but very little of it makes any sense outside the context of committed community.

To treat the *Rule* as instruction for personal spirituality apart from community is to sever the tree from its roots. With Benedictine spirituality—as with any expression of Christianity—the context is other people, and the context is critical.

The monastery—a residential worshiping community with limited exposure to the rest of the world—is just an especially radical (or clear or pure) example of the almost totally forgotten truth that Christianity is communal. You cannot come close to authentically following Jesus or obeying the teachings of Jesus all by yourself.

Jesus says love one another. You can't do that alone.

Jesus says forgive one another. You can't do that alone.

Jesus says serve one another. That requires another.

Jesus says share your resources with one another. It's impossible to share money with yourself. That's not sharing. That's keeping.

In fact, regarding the individual as distinct from the greater community would have seemed foreign to Benedict. He rarely speaks of individualism in a positive way.

Examples of the critical role of community in the individual's development are abundant. Spiritual growth happens as the monks "serve one another," "quietly encourage each other," bless and receive blessings from one another, "try to be the first to show respect to the other," "support with the greatest patience one another's weaknesses," "compete . . . with one another" in obedience, and even "pursue what [they judge] better for" the other.[40]

In his commentary on Benedict's great chapter on humility, Hubert van Zeller writes, "Community life spells [what is required]" to "the humble man."[41] In other words, God uses the committed, consistent presence of others to shape and grow the individual into the image of Christ.

Christianity happens with others. It is a distinctly others-focused religion. That fact is especially obvious in a monastery, where a few specific people commit to eating, sleeping, working, and praying together for the rest of their lives.

Is community the goal? No. Salvation is the goal. Restoration of all things is the goal.

But what a monastery reveals very clearly is that restoration happens best within the context of stable community. The monks are there for one another. Similarly, for us Christians living outside of the monastery, the primary reason for our being in a place is not ourselves; it is others.

We are here for you.

Prioritize the Reasons to Stay

When I spent part of a summer living with Benedictine monks, one of my goals was to learn how monastic community, fortified by the vow of stability, could be translated to and embraced by non-monastic, modern Christian church communities.

Like many before me, I had grown increasingly frustrated by the erosion of the North American church: the vacuous liturgies, the self-help sermons, all the entertainment. I carried difficult questions and was searching the monastic tradition for answers.

My burning curiosity was this: could the monks share with me something that "didn't seem to want to be shared, but only joined."[42] Could something core to the monastic life be the remedy for malnourished modern Christians? Could the secret strength of this ancient form translate to another culture? In other words, could the modern American church embrace and experience stability?

One of the surprises of my summer was that most of the monks of whom I asked this question responded by saying simply, "No. You can't. Not in the modern church and especially not in America." In fact, one of the common reasons the monks gave for why they themselves initially joined the monastery was that they were looking for stable Christian community and had not found it in the church.

There are several reasons why they hadn't found it in the church (and they weren't shy about pointing them out) but the main reason the American church had failed to be a stable environment for spiritual growth was this: the church is saturated with consumerism.

This was a theme I'd considered before. In much of North American culture, we treat the church less like a community and more like a commodity. We see the church less like a family that you stick with through thick and thin and more like a phone company which you drop the second there's a better offer from another. The problem isn't with the church, really. The problem is with the way most of us relate with the church.

Church is built on Christ and the teachings of his apostles. That's a solid foundation. However, the church community is made up of a bunch of regular folks like you and me who are usually driven more by convenience than commitment, who prefer ease to effort, who are pretty good at noticing what's wrong but not so good at being grateful for what's right . . .

with this church . . .

with this house . . .

with this marriage . . .

with this job . . .

with this moment in time . . .

In a sermon on the value of community, my friend Stephanie noted, "There's always a reason to leave." She said, "Having a reason to leave is easy." But, "simply having a reason is not reason enough."

The value of consumerism says, "You need the newer, you deserve the better; there's always a reason to leave." The value of stability says, "Let's prioritize the reasons to stay."

The monks might be right. Without a doubt the modern church is crippled by consumerism. Several monks I talked to shared that their decision to become a monk was directly and specifically connected to their specific monastery. Their commitment to community was not a hypothetical or abstract ideal. They made vows to live life in this place with these men. The attraction wasn't to being a monk or to monasticism in general. What compelled them to join the monastery was the hope of sharing life and pursuing Jesus in this community. But maybe the answer—at least for many of us—is not to join a monastery.

Maybe the answer for us is to work to restore the church—to choose to be a stabilizing communal presence in the midst of a very unstable, individualistic culture. Maybe the answer for us is to value staying in this moment, in this place, in this relationship, in this community, instead of getting caught up in the bigger cultural current of constant change. . . .

If we did that—if we valued stability even in the midst of a constantly changing culture—what would happen?

1) *Valuing stability would counter the pursuit of a "perfect church."*

What fuels much of the consumerism in the church is the false ideal of the perfect church. Now, you can chase that ideal—of "everything as I like it"—or you can choose a very different guiding value, which is stability. And then the fact that this church isn't perfect becomes unremarkable. And the response to the inevitable critique of some portion of the church becomes, "Oh yeah, I know. But I'm not playing that game anymore."

This is not to say that we neglect the need to improve things or that we grow apathetic or that we become accepting of mediocrity. It's simply to say that consistent, stable, enduring relationships with others in the community become more valuable than the "perfect" worship band, the "perfect" preacher, or the "perfect" youth program.

What would happen if we valued relational stability in the midst of a constantly changing culture?

2) *Valuing stability would counter the illusion of a "perfect marriage."*

Stability doesn't mean you're not trying to improve or that you don't work on the problems. Just the opposite. It means you know you're going to work hard, and you expect problems. This isn't a fairy tale. This is learning how to love.

If we valued stability, we'd worry less about creating a perfect family. We'd have a different definition of a "good home." We might have a real sense of peace about a less-than-perfect job. Because valuing stability is different from valuing more . . . and it's more than valuing me.

People who believe stability matters and has value are usually motivated by the wellbeing of others. As the apostle

John writes, "It has given me great joy to find some of your children walking in the truth" (2 John 4).

Clearly there are personal benefits to stability. But sometimes the fact that "this will be good for me" isn't motivating enough. What keeps me from running away from hard things is believing that my staying will be good for someone else.

What if the value of stability is not just something you'd embrace "for your sake" but is something you might consider embracing "for the sake of others"? What kind of impact could your life have on the lives of others if they knew—if they truly believed—that the reason you were there was for them?

Stability is not the icing on the relational cake. It is essential. Stability is a necessary base ingredient of any relationship that truly matters. Stability is foundational. The assurance that you are committed to being here and staying here with me, through pains and joys, is what makes meaningful and transformational community possible. This is the quality of community we long for. It grows from the root of stability.

But I Don't Like Conflict

This sounds great! So why is it so rare?

Because of conflict. Because it's hard. Because we're not getting along right now. Because he's so critical of me. Because she doesn't appreciate my effort. Because I'm not being fed. Because my kids don't like the teacher. Because: conflict.

There's always been conflict. Conflict is part of life. There will be a lot more conflict in the days to come.

I don't like conflict. You probably don't either. But every good story has conflict. Every good story is about a character who wants something and has to overcome conflict to get it. So rather than running away from conflict—does that even work?—we could spend our energy working to overcome it. And the way we start is by staying. We choose to stay because it is the only way to communicate, in action, that this conflict will not make me run. This conflict will be faced and, in time, will be worked through and overcome.

Let me just name the variable that is swirling all around this conversation about stability. It's risk.[43] It's risking that staying will be worth it. It's risking that a life marked by stability is more meaningful—in the end—than a life marked by consumerism.

It is risky. It is not guaranteed. There may be real and lasting disappointments. You might get hurt. You might get hurt again. You're going to lose some. Like Jacob, who wrestles with the God who is not somewhere else, you might walk with a limp for the rest of your days. This whole stability thing is risky. Of course it is.

Is the potential payoff worth the risk? That's the decision you need to make.

This could go bad. Yes. It could. It could also become beautiful. It could all be restored. It could be really, really good. Committing to stay is taking a risk. That's the choice you need to make.

You have three options.

- 1: You could leave. You could choose to exit the relationship.
- 2: You could succumb. You could perpetually take the hit. You could pretend that the conflict isn't happening or that it doesn't hurt, and you could just give in, over and over.
- 3: You could work for restoration. Acknowledging the brokenness and the need for health and wholeness, you could resolve to put things back together.

With Option 1 you lose the relationship. With Option 2 you lose your soul. But Option 3 reflects the Benedictine vow of stability. Option 3 reflects a greater motivation than the simple avoidance of conflict. It understands that conflict is fertile ground for growth. Option 3 holds out hope for redemption. Option 3 takes seriously the power of the resurrection. Option 3 refuses to quit or to succumb and faces conflict, instead, with these life-changing words: "Or, we could restore all things."

"This is what will end it for me," I once told my dad in a moment of unguarded transparency.

"What, exactly?" he asked, surprised to hear any mention of my quitting the pastorate. He assumed he had missed something. He knew ministry was my passion, my calling, the work for which I'd trained and the only work I'd ever done. He knew how zealous I'd been in our work to start and build a church.

"People leaving," I said, quietly. "Someday I'll get a call from someone and it'll just be the last time I can take it. I'll pack up my books and move to a cabin in Montana."

Now, hopefully, my retirement won't actually be a self-preserving admission of defeat. I pray I'll have greater fortitude and wisdom when the time comes. But that whole "people leaving" part of being a pastor of a church, no matter how many times I'm reminded that "it's just part of ministry," or chided for not having "thick skin"—it just kills me.

Because it feels like personal rejection? I'm sure that's part of it, though it shouldn't be.

Because you need their help? Of course, we always need help. All communities have needs and few are helped by people leaving.

But most of all because leaving erodes the foundation of community, which is stability.

A basic requirement for any effective family, community, or organization is stability. At the end of the day, we need people who consistently show up, who are there, and who will remain.

I remember participating with my kids one year in a fledgling youth sports program. The season was a disaster. At more than half the games the opposing team didn't even show up. After a few big disappointments our own players' commitments waned, and soon we were the team without enough kids to play. I don't know of anyone who played in that league the following season. Folks opted for leagues with an established level of commitment. This was yet another example in our lives that made the lesson clear: In order to function at a basic level, teams and families and companies and clubs and church communities need to be able to count on one thing: that you will be there.

You may think I'm overstating the severity of the effects of joining and then leaving a church. But I'm sure Benedict wouldn't. Lifelong commitment to his community was a prerequisite! He saw stability as the essential foundation of meaningful community.

It's not the work-related moves out of town or the carefully considered vision-driven departures that hurt. Of course, there are good and healthy reasons to leave a church community that should be respected and even celebrated. Those exits may be grieved but they typically cause minimal damage. What absolutely erodes the local church is when participants become spectators, investors devolve into takers, and those once willing to share the burden of responsibility stop working to address problems and choose instead to point them out as an excuse to leave.

Today, we celebrate consumerism and we even consume the church. We take what we want until we're no longer interested, and then we move on. If there's a better offer down the road, we're quick to make the switch. It's remarkable to me how little commitment I sense in people about where they "go to church." It's like we're talking about a restaurant they may frequent, not a family for which they are willing to sacrifice.

The late Trappist monk Francis Kline asks, "How can anything produce something else if the connections are pulled away? If we pull away emotionally from our unpleasant situation . . . we must leave and begin again, working very hard to accomplish no more than we did the last time. A similar situation will form itself a second time, and the cycle will begin all over."[44]

How This Relates to My Marriage

Easily the most unexpected benefit of spending a few weeks at the monastery that summer was the renewed vision for my marriage that the monks gave me. Here's how it happened.

In conversations with several monks, plus others who were visiting for extended seasons of discerning whether or not to join the community, I asked, "Why?" "Why did you become (or are you considering becoming) a monk?"

Most of these young men were in their twenties. They were from Poland and Germany and all over the United States. Their stories were unique and totally fascinating. But there was one phrase I kept hearing over and over. It was, "This is a good life."

"Why are you contemplating becoming a monk?" I would ask. And they would pause and then thoughtfully respond. And nearly everyone included, as part of their answer, this simple phrase: "This is a good life."

They didn't mean it in a "we've arrived" sense, or in the way people refer to some ideal as "the life." They were simply stating their conviction that this—an avowed commitment to obeying God with these people in this place—was a good way to live.

At first, I didn't think much about it. But I kept hearing it: from the old monk who walked slowly down the rock stairs and handed me his cane before sitting down to talk with me . . .

to the brilliant PhD student from Notre Dame . . . to the tall twenty-something from Poland with a deep voice and a tragic past. "This is a good life."

I became more and more challenged by this phrase because it revealed a perspective which, on a practical level, I don't often embrace. It's not that I don't love my life. I do. It's that much of the time my mind wanders into the "what ifs" surrounding the activities of the past weeks, or the "what ifs" surrounding big decisions of the past decades.

What if I had made a different choice at that critical point of transition? What if I had taken that job? What if we had stayed in that town?

I often hear myself saying, "This is a good summer," while thinking mostly about what I like about this summer and how next summer I'll do something different. Or I'll say, "It's been a good year," while thinking about projects I've committed to this year and different projects I may take up next year. But here were these men who had made, or were about to make, a whole life commitment to serving God in this specific community, with these specific people. Not just this summer, but all year, every year, for their whole life.

Their embrace of stability had quieted the retrospective voices of doubt or regret—the relentless "what ifs" and restless wondering. Their embrace of stability freed them from the all-too-common, half-hearted engagement in the present that results from always trying to keep your future options open.

I found myself challenged by their perspective: their resolute commitment to permanence alongside their profound sense of freedom. I was moved by this deep joy that I saw as they expressed their complete surrender of themselves for the sake of God and others. "This is a good life" they said, as if the value of consumerism had finally been shaken off, as if the blinders of individualism had been thrown away.

They weren't referring specifically to what they wanted in life or what they liked about monasticism. They were speaking, instead, of a kind of contentment. Theirs was a joyful surrender to a greater pursuit—one worthy enough of complete devotion. This is a meaningful life, they were saying, a life worth living.

It was actually somewhat jarring to hear young guys in their twenties not talking about "taking a year off to travel" or "trying this out for a while" but making a lifelong vow of stability to these people and this place and this way. I was inspired as I listened to them refer to their whole life in terms of a single choice—a challenging choice and maybe even a difficult choice, but ultimately a good choice.

The challenge came in sensing their contentment with their decision—the almost ironic sense of freedom rooted in that vow, in that commitment to stay here for an entire lifetime.

As a result, what I began to think about in these moments was my marriage. I thought, for example, of the early days when we were just naïve twenty-three-year-olds, the painful times, the early losses, the joy of children, the challenges of parenting, the setbacks and disappointments, the daily responsibilities and the driving and the bills and the house projects and so many other ways I could have spent the last two-and-a-half decades of my life.

And I thought about how, most of the time, when I think about my marriage, I think about what I think is going well with this relationship or what's not going well, what's good or not so good about my marriage from my perspective, about what I like and what I don't like, about what's hard about it, what's wonderful about it for me.

I evaluate it. I kind of analyze it. And of course, some of that is important because I want to address problems and get better, and of course all relationships take work and working on relationships is a good thing, and so the analysis continues.

But what if I just embraced it? What if I accepted the married life and the wife to which I'm vowed not as "part of my life" but as the life to which I am called, and furthermore, as good.

This is a good life.

A lot of the time, in these critical moments of analysis and evaluation, I'm looking at this most significant, most meaningful human relationship in my life and thinking of the commitment of stability for my sake. I'm thinking about how I feel about all these real-life challenges and opportunities . . . about a thousand different choices that I need to make and how they'll affect me.

What I sensed in the lives of these monks was not that their vow of stability was easy, but that it was deeply settled. They were fully surrendered to the long-term nature of it.

And so am I. I am all in. There's no confusion on that point.

But in the middle of the craziness of a Tuesday morning, I become so critical . . . of everything. I get critical because I'm thinking about me. I'm thinking about how I feel. I'm not thinking about others. What talking with these young men reminded me of was that, in fact, I have made a vow of stability for the sake of another. It's my marriage vow.

I don't have to navigate how I feel about a thousand different decisions. I just have to wholeheartedly embrace the one decision I made nearly twenty-five years ago to live this one life with this one person. I have made a lifelong vow to this person. And this is a good life.

Marriage may be challenging and difficult. It will certainly require lots of growth and honesty and better communication. Some days will be amazing, and some days will be not so amazing. And we'll always be working on that. But the degree to which marriage is challenging or easy is not the point. The point is simply that this is my life and it's good. It's completely worthy of my full resolve for my entire lifetime.

My spiritual director's summary of the Benedictine ethic is, "My brother is my life."[45] Not part of my life. Not a piece of the context in which my life happens. Is. My brother is my life. This monastic example serves every Christian in general. Monks call all Christians to live a radically others-focused life. But specifically, in regard to my particular situation, Carmen is my life. Not a beautiful part of it. Not part of the context in which my life happens. Is. My wife is my life.

Rock solid stability and wholehearted, singularly focused devotion to this life in the domestic monastery of our marriage is my calling. This is my vow. And that's how monks helped my marriage.

Relational Stability Has So Many Benefits

The ramifications of relational stability—between husbands and wives, and in families of all kinds—are revealed over generations. When a person is raised outside the context of a stable family, they naturally seek that sense of stability in others. An unmet need for stability is sometimes so intense that it sabotages relationships. A person struggles to find the footing on which to build meaningful connections. But when someone experiences a legitimate sense of stability with their family of origin, they are given the ability to belong and to function as a healthy, secure part of a greater whole. Stability experienced in family enables future stability. The stable home is the foundation from which a person develops emotionally, spiritually, relationally, financially, and socially.

While families who value and practice stability may not appear to be doing anything especially remarkable, they are in fact equipping their children for healthy future relationships. On the other hand, homes which lack stability end up contributing to a person's perpetual search for a sense of belonging. Whether it's sticking with a team through a tough season, staying in a marriage through tragedy, or persevering as a monk in a monastery, the basic capacity to integrate and thrive and not bail out is formed, to a significant degree, early in life within the context of the family.

I think you'll find great joy in embracing your relationships as the context for practicing stability. Whether in a church, a marriage, or a home, stability in relationships is an exercise in endurance—but the benefits are tangibly felt. There is likely no greater adversity to stability than the daily, real-life challenge of sharing life with others for the long haul. The challenge is so great, in fact, that we will almost certainly give up unless our motivation for sticking with it is something/ someone greater than ourselves.

Stability is pursued, at first, for my sake. It addresses my formation and the restless longings in my heart. I need to stay because I need to stay. I need to put down roots. I need to grow and be pruned and become healthy. So, I stay for my sake. But then things shift: stability continues to help me, but it also becomes a value I embrace for the sake of others. I choose to stay for their formation, to address the restless longings in their hearts, to provide security and freedom for them to become healthy.

Initially, the value of stability is personal. Then it becomes a value I hold for others. I need to stay, not just for me. I need to stay for them. The deeper I lean into stability the more my life becomes others-focused. The inverse is true as well: the more I focus on others the more important stability will become to me. And then comes the joy.

Near the end of his life, the Apostle John writes a few short letters that are included in the Bible. In one, called 2 John— it's just thirteen verses—he's writing to a small church, and he says: "It has given me great joy to find some of your children walking in the truth, just as the Father commanded us" (v. 4).

This is interesting, because most of the letters in Scripture are written to the first generation of Christ-followers. The instruction is to them, for them. But later in his life John is writing to the church, and it's no longer just about them. It's about their kids. It's about the next generation. It's about others.

The steadfast faith of his community has spawned and sustained more spiritual life. John's long endurance is fueled, he seems to say, by the joy of seeing the fruit of his generation's stability. Their roots have grown deep and their branches are reaching wide, and now many others are finding shelter in their strength. These are the beauties to be experienced in lives of stability.

Journal

Second Week at the Monastery

I'm wondering if all this praying could become self-centered, in a surprising way. There's lots of self-analysis and personal language. There's also some intercession. Most of my prayer is intercession, normally.

After Prime I walk the mile down the mountain into the town of Norcia. It's a sad, beat-up place. The earthquakes did so much damage. Most of the houses and nearly all the businesses I pass are destroyed.

In the early afternoon I'm invited to sit and talk with Fr. M., whose face and voice are immensely kind. We discuss a variety of things before landing on the vow of stability. He says stability is rooted in the fact that God doesn't change. Then he says, "I need to be able to be stable in one place long enough to unpack the stability of God, the nature of God." He says, "Stability enables the encounter of divine love."

It's nearing the next time for prayer, but because I feel so entirely comfortable with Fr. M., I share my morning musings about so much prayer becoming self-centered. I confess that in just a few days, I've prayed for everybody I can think to pray for. I don't want to admit it, but I'm struggling with all these hours devoted to prayer.

He says, "The answer to your question is adoration. The monk's main job is to adore God. The more adoration, the more purity. The more purity, the more effective the intercession."

The monk's simple response reveals a critical flaw in my prayer life. Prayer, for me, has slowly become a series of tasks: pray for her, pray for him, pray for them. . . . Once the tasks are complete, doing them again, just a few hours later, feels unnecessary. But adoring God? There's plenty of room in my life for more adoration. And there can never be too much adoration. I'm humbled. But I'm ready to go back to prayer.

The next day, I'm missing Carmen terribly. It's a gift to talk on the phone, but it also pulls me out of the focus of this place in a way that is a bit difficult for me to navigate. I'm married, so there will always be that double focus. It's made very clear in a place like this how much time and energy is spent on family, work, and so many of the "basics" of a "normal life."

Here's the schedule the monks follow:
4 hours of prayer
4 hours of reading
4–6 hours of working
1 hour of eating
8 hours of sleeping
About 1 hour of transition time.

I've now been at the monastery for one week! Feels longer! I wonder if one of the reasons time seems to move slowly here is that I'm more present to the moment, because I'm pausing so often for prayer. It may have to do with the fact that I'm getting out of bed at 3:10 a.m. and fasting most of the day.

I've begun spending most of the afternoons writing in the ruins of an old monastery carved into the mountainside near the current chapel and chapter house. There's just enough shelter from the sun and occasional rain in this makeshift office.

I'm remembering the tomb of St. Francis (which my family and I visited in Assisi several weeks ago) and how three of Francis's closest friends were buried near him. These were men who faithfully stood beside him through the difficulties of life's trials. I've heard the phrase "your bury-a-body buddy" as a reference to the guy you can call anytime, no questions asked, to help you with whatever you need, even if what you need is to "bury a body." A more beautiful and compelling image is the image of a "buddy" so devoted to you that he would ask for his body to be buried near yours. How powerful to imagine that stability in relationships in this life could become so profoundly meaningful that one's hope for eternity would include the continued presence of that relationship.

I typically say, "I'll take a break to pray." Monks take a break from prayer to do anything else.

Praying so regularly has revealed some things. . . . It's much easier to focus when I'm praying once a day for five or ten minutes. My mind has wandered a lot during prayer here.

Another factor is the repetition of the form: stand up, sit down, glorias, etc.

Another factor is being so hungry in the morning. We pray at:

3:30 a.m. for an hour.

6 a.m. for thirty minutes.

7:45 a.m. for fifteen minutes.

10 a.m. for fifteen minutes.

Followed by Mass for an hour, and again at 12:45 p.m. for fifteen minutes—all before we eat the first meal! That's six prayer times and ten hours before we eat. These guys are warriors pursuing a life of devotion!

What am I pursuing?

CHAPTER 4
Stability and Place
Shaped by the Land

"A tree cannot bear fruit
if it is often transplanted."

—BENEDICTA WARD[46]

In the middle of the fourth century, near the Nile River Valley in Egypt, a large African man named Moses the Black led a group of bandits known for terrorizing the region with violence.

Once, after committing a crime, Moses hid from local authorities in a monastic colony in Skete, in the Western desert near Alexandria. This was not a single house where monks lived together, but a colony of monks living in proximity to one another in small single rooms or "cells." So, as he hid for days among the cells, Moses observed the monks and was impressed by their sense of peace and contentment. He soon returned, renounced his old way of life, and became a monk himself.

But being a monk wasn't easy for Moses. He struggled with how slowly his life changed. He wanted to be holy, but the

journey toward holiness was slow and arduous and he didn't
see a lot of progress. More than once, he concluded that he
just wasn't able to pursue God as a monk. But each time he
faltered, Moses would be encouraged by an older monk to
trust God, be graceful to himself, and continue the journey.

Eventually Moses became the leader of the community in
Skete. And when Moses was seventy-five years old, another
group of violent bandits attacked the monastery. Some of the
monks wanted to take up arms, but Moses urged them against
it. He told them to flee and that he and a few others would
attempt to welcome the attackers with grace as he, himself,
had been welcomed long ago. Moses, and those who stayed
with him, were martyred. He is still remembered today as a
man who was truly changed—as a violent man who became
holy.

Moses the Black is perhaps best known for this word of
instruction which he gave to a young man who came to him
looking for spiritual counsel. Abbot Moses said, "Go, sit in
your cell, and your cell will teach you everything."[47]

How Does That Work?

What no one seems to have recorded is what the young man
did with this pithy bit of advice. I wonder if, on his way back
down the mountain, he scratched his head in bewilderment.
I wonder if he concluded his quest was pure folly. Why did
he expect to receive any practical life guidance from a monk?
What was he to do with this? "Go, sit in your cell . . ."

Really?

The brilliance of Abbot Moses's words, which may, at first
glance, sound hopelessly simplistic, is hidden in the *realness* of
place: the physicality of a place, the specificity of a place, the
limitations of a place, the difficulties of a place.

Learning requires a *place*. The fact that learning "takes place" in a real location is significant. The harder-to-define spiritual realities for which humanity has always searched—experiences like peace and purpose, joy and security, which transcend space—are almost always tied to a specific place. At least initially. The good abbot knew that.

"Go, sit in your cell, and your cell will teach you everything." In fact, it's difficult to identify anything of significance which I've learned that is not, in some integral way, linked to a place.

Take, for example, the deep and powerful sense of being grounded, of belonging, which I experienced when I returned home from my first year of college on Christmas break. The house and property where I grew up was where I first experienced a fledgling version of the real and robust sense of security which now regularly accompanies my soul wherever I go. I first learned it there, in that specific place.

My current sense of security isn't about a place. It supersedes place. But I wonder if I would have ever really come to know it without that place. So much of what I've learned is linked to the land. "As I've traveled the world for @natgeo trying to understand the emotional fallout of environmental change," writes *National Geographic* photographer Pete Muller, "I've thought a lot about the way our minds make meaning. In some ways, our physical surroundings are arbitrary. It's *what happens to us there* that matters."[48]

The most plain, basic, and obvious application of the value of stability is a physical place: a room or a cell, a specific house, an actual neighborhood, a city with a name like Lincoln, California, or Lansing, Michigan, or wherever it is on the map that your life is occupying space and taking place. Wherever you *are*. Wherever, for you, is *here*.

The original and immediate meaning of Benedict's vow of stability was to live steadfastly in the monastery until death.

The monastery was the workshop for the soul, and in order to get soul work done, one needed to stay in the workshop. You needed to remain in that place. You vowed to stay right where you were. The conviction that you had a permanent home in God was expressed by staying in one place with one community of people.

In other words, there are a lot of really important factors in our lives, and one of them is place. This simple thing we call "here"—with all its nuanced complexities and specific difficulties—is where the learning happens. And "here" is where we need what we learn to make a real difference.

Last year I flew to Charlottesville, Virginia, to spend a few days with one of my best friends. We met in college, we were in each other's weddings, and we've remained close through lots of joys and a few sorrows for over twenty-five years.

Sometime over the last couple of decades, both of us, without knowing it about the other, starting reading—and being shaped by—The Rule of St. Benedict.

Once, while on a video call with Greg, I noticed a familiar picture in the background on the wall of his office; he confirmed it was an icon of St. Benedict . . . the very same image I had hanging on my office wall. Greg then shared how he, with a few others in his community, had been following a Benedictine Rule of life for years. They had adapted Benedict's ancient *Rule* for monastic life and were living it out in their modern, non-monastic church community and in their neighborhoods throughout Charlottesville.

I was in the midst of researching modern adaptations of the *Rule* myself. In recent months I had traveled to Italy and various cities in the US to witness ways it was being applied today. So it wasn't long before I flew to Virginia. I wanted to learn from Greg in Charlottesville—the town where he and his wife went to graduate school, built a house, were raising their four children, and were pastoring a big Presbyterian church.

They were deeply embedded in the fabric of their community. When others in this highly mobile culture had moved on, they had remained. Their roots had grown deep and strong. This place had shaped them, nourished, and challenged them. As a result of their stability—their lived-out commitment to being *here*—their lives were now bearing good fruit.

The first thing Greg said to me when he pulled up to the curb at the airport was, "I should warn you: things are very tense at home."

"Really?" I responded. "Are the kids OK?"

"We just told them we're moving."

Stunned, I sat in silence, and then began to slowly reflect on the irony. I had traveled across the country to study stability but would end up spending the weekend helping my friend and his family pack their home into boxes. I went to discuss the power of staying but we mostly talked about leaving. The plan was to dig into the dynamics of living life in one place, but the bulk of our time was spent getting ready for a move to another place. All of this contributed to the paradoxical conviction that the place is super important but that it's not ultimately about the place.

When Abbot Moses said to the young brother, "Go, sit in your cell, and your cell will teach you everything," he meant that the cell was the tutor, not the end goal.

What Does Here Teach?

Greg and his family are fine, but this was part of my learning about place and here. If place is the tutor, what does it teach me? What does it teach any of us who are patient enough to learn from it?

Who I Am

Many ingredients over many years mix and ferment to form the complex wonder of one's identity. The role of place is to keep it real. It's the rubber-meets-the-road dynamic of a specific place that both *guards* against an overly imagined perspective of oneself and *reveals* one's actual power.

For instance, I may think of myself as an effective leader, but the truth will be borne out in the place where I live. Am I a loving father? My home will tell you. Am I a good neighbor? Ask those who share my street. Do I bring order or chaos? Check my closet. Do I give life and love to others? Sit at my table. Place is the container of reality.

The Benedictine rule of stability is not a piece of idealism; it is practical and realistic, and it takes form most acutely in life's literal locations. Esther de Waal writes, "Without stability we cannot know our true selves. For we are pulled apart by so many conflicting demands, so many things deserving of our attention, that often it seems as though the center cannot hold."

She argues that we are "confused and superficial."[49]

Nothing cuts through the superficiality of the presented self like the reality of one's place. Nothing grounds us and holds the "center" together quite like our place. Applying flattering filters to our lives is far less convenient in the real place where we live than in the virtual spaces where we present curated images. There's no off switch to being a neighbor. We can't just cover up the rough edges of our personalities in our homes. Truth is on full display *in that place*. The place mirrors back what's real. And in that sense the place becomes the teacher.

How I'm Affected

Second, place teaches me how I'm affected. This subtle dynamic is easily missed but so important to recognize: I am affected by my surroundings. What's outside affects what's inside. I am shaped by place. The context in which a seed is planted is not the same thing as the seed, but it does affect the seed.

I've read about how minerals and other elements in soils can affect the flavors of the fruits grown in that soil and can even affect the flavors of the meat harvested from the animals who eat the grass that comes from that soil. What's outside affects what's inside.

I once spent a whole summer during college living and working in the Uptown neighborhood in inner-city Chicago. I'd spend most of the day with twenty or thirty elementary-aged kids who lived in a homeless shelter in a concrete warehouse with no windows. I'd sleep every night in an old hotel room with ten other guys. *Ten!* My context—the space in which life was happening—was always hot, crowded, dirty, and chaotic. And it impacted me. I was not the space, but I was definitely *in* the space, and the space affected me. It shaped and influenced me.

Every few days I'd get a break from work and I'd walk about thirty minutes, cross Lake Shore Drive, and sit on the edge of Lake Michigan. I'd take off my shoes and let the water cool my feet. With my back to the city all I could see before me was a shimmering blue-green oasis. My body would breathe in fresh air and my mind would quiet down and my soul would feel renewed.

I don't remember a time in my life when I was more aware of my environment or of the impact my environment was having on my soul and on me. This awareness was instructive. I was learning how my person is affected by my place, how my environment impacts my feelings and my actions. I continue to experience the very personal effects of place to this day, when I walk into a cluttered closet or open the door to a beautiful sanctuary or sit in bumper-to-bumper traffic.

Being affected by place is, in and of itself, neither good nor bad. The influence of an environment can be healthy, neutral, or destructive. The specific ways I was affected by the windowless homeless shelter or the old hotel room or the beautiful lake is not the point. The point is simply recognizing that what's outside affects what's inside. That simple recognition turns the place into a teacher . . . one which helps us learn how we are affected.

What is it about me that hungers for open spaces? Why do I become defensive and critical instead of loving and graceful when the room feels chaotic? Can I become a person who can enter into a space without being controlled by it? How could I, myself, become a stabilizing presence wherever I go?

These are such critical lessons to learn but they cannot be learned hypothetically. These are practical lessons, so these lessons take place. They require the instructional power of a specific space. Our place, wherever it is, can become a powerful teacher, showing us how we are affected by physical realities of the space around us.

What I Need

Third, place teaches me what I need (and don't need).

St. Benedict's strong criticism of gyrovagues was that they were "always on the move, they never settle down, and are slaves to their own wills and gross appetites."[50] It's their constant moving, their unwillingness to remain in one place, which keeps them from discovering even a basic understanding of themselves. They spend their whole lives pursuing their wants and desires—their "own wills and gross appetites"—never slowing down long enough to learn what they truly need.

Always on the hunt for something different or easier, something more exciting or sweeter to feed their addiction, they tragically overlook the true source of lasting fulfillment. They never stay, and so they never learn what they really need.

Their dissatisfaction, which is still so commonly experienced in today's always-moving culture, fuels their ongoing search. But the fruit they're seeking eludes them, not because it's always moving but because they are. Stability's fruit blooms where it's planted. It thrives where it's nurtured. But most never stick around long enough to taste it. We are habituated to believe, argues Jonathan Wilson-Hartgrove, cofounder of a neo-monastic community, that the answer to our questions is always somewhere else.[51] We have been trained by an economy of planned obsolescence and a culture of fast fashion to ditch the old and move on to the new, and the sooner, the better.

All this moving and shopping and consuming and upgrading has honed our sense of what we like. But we're really confused about what we need.

"Here," writes de Waal, "is a fundamental human need. We need a place." Why? Because place is instructive. She continues, "Everyone needs to feel at home, to feel earthed, for it is impossible to say, 'Who am I?' without first asking, 'Where am I? Whence have I come? Where am I going?'"[52]

Several years ago, I worked alongside Christian refugees who had fled their own country due to persecution but were illegally residing in Thailand. They were stateless. They had no citizenship. They had no home. What many in my world seem to take for granted—a place to be, a place to root, a place to return—was absent for them. I took note when they shared that it was not the struggle for food or shelter that took the greatest toll, but the inescapable feeling that they were "strangers everywhere." They had no roots to a place. They were "unearthed."

It seems to me that it is *remaining* in a place for a long time, or, on the other hand, being forced to live for a long time *without* a place, that teaches us what we need and what we really don't need, the difference between what's essential and what really boils down to preference or even entertainment.

The modern American gyrovague never develops beyond their preferences. Their place-related questions never mature beyond the most elementary, "Do I like this place?" And so, place remains always something to be consumed. It is not honored as a revealer of truth. It is not served as valuable or stewarded as critical to life. When there are no roots in the ground the place becomes superfluous, inconsequential, unnecessary. We just use the place. We don't learn from it. But when we choose to stay, when we remain in a place (or maybe, for some, when we wish we could stay but are forced to leave), the place pulses with significance. It becomes a powerful teacher.

I was once helping my mom set granite rocks in just the right places in her front yard flower garden. We had gathered the stones from around the property which my parents have cultivated for decades. We talked about the rocks as we struggled to move them from a rusty red wheelbarrow into the newly turned soil. We talked about them in a way that was different than if we had purchased them from the local landscaping supply yard. "Everything means something," she commented, "the trees, the dirt, the rocks, everything, when you've lived in the same place for forty years."

What she was referring to, by "everything," was more than her sense of familiarity with these few acres of land, more than the sense of accomplishment she felt from planting orchards or growing flowers. By "everything" she quite literally meant her life, which, though not unaffected by grief and pain, is pulsing with meaning. In this place, where she has stayed, where her roots have plunged deep, where her life has borne fruit, she can point to real examples of practical provision and lasting goodness. She can tell stories of sweet memories and loving relationships. In this place, surrounded by three acres and forty years of perspective, she has learned what she needs and what she doesn't.

What I Want

Fourth, place teaches me what I want.

I don't mean to assign every desire to the ethical doghouse, as if the good life is one which rejects all passion. There's a difference between the frivolous and self-centered consumerism that Benedict associates with gyrovagues, and the deep, true, resonant longings of our hearts.

The question "What do you want?" is, after all, perhaps the most important of spiritual questions. Author and spiritual director Margaret Guenther begins her book *My Soul in Silence Waits* with a chapter titled "Longing," in which she reflects on the importance of knowing what you want.[53]

To distinguish lesser wants (she mentions, as examples, a "piece of cake" and a "window seat in an airplane") from deeper, truer wants, Guenther shifts the question slightly from "What do you want?" to "What do you love?"[54] She's inviting the reader to work through the clutter of relative affluence— all the stuff, all the options, all that is so readily available to us—in order to identify and name what we truly desire, what we actually love enough to prioritize and pursue.

Years ago, I took Guenther's little book to a cabin in the Northwoods of Wisconsin where I planned to spend two weeks slowly working through all eight chapters. I never made it past the first. It's not so much that I got stuck on this question. It's that I needed to stay with this question for a while. I needed to sit with this question, not in the nebulous, hypothetical realm of ideas, but in the actual, physical reality of a place. The place keeps my answers honest. The place would ground me to the real.

What do you want? To honestly answer this question requires great discernment and even greater effort. Arriving at some satisfying level of clarity may take some time, and, I would argue, will almost certainly require some *space*. It's your *place*—it's where you are that will help you recognize what you really want.

When I'm away from home I realize, with renewed clarity, what I love about where I live. When I'm away from my family, the little quirks and annoyances that often irritate me fade away and I miss what's true and unique and good about each of them. And a similar dynamic is at play when I'm *here*, when I'm *not* away. It's just a bit more difficult to notice. But when I pay attention to this place—to where I am—one of the things that clarifies is what I want, what I truly want, what I love enough to prioritize.

What I Should Do

Fifth and finally, place teaches me what I should do.

It's the specific needs, resources, and opportunities of the place that clarify my purpose. Like everyone, I long for a meaningful vocation, for a role to play that will make a difference. But that desire remains theoretical and conceptual and ultimately unfulfilled until it locks into an actual place.

I remember the point in graduate school when I realized I simply could not write another paper about ministry. I couldn't design another hypothetical strategy for an imagined situation. I was becoming exhausted by assignments requiring me to "describe how you might respond in a scenario with the following factors. . . ."

I loved my time in school, and I'm grateful for the training I received almost every day. I learned from incredible instructors and mentors. My formal education was a worthwhile investment of time and money. But I could only go so far in the academy. To move from philosophical concept to action required an actual location. And it wouldn't be enough to just read about it. I needed to go there.

Initially, the move from graduate school to the first city in which we ministered was shocking. My first memory is of a gathering of several young couples, which, on the surface, looked like the kind of "place" we'd been living for years. But instead of the familiar and common-to-graduate-school conversational topics like ideas, theology, relationships, and future plans, all these guys talked about for an hour was the (then) Oakland Raiders. Most of them worked in construction and had never attended college. These were good people, and we were blessed to share life with them. But our purpose needed to be contextualized to that place. In order for us to know what to do *here*, we needed to stay here for a while, and we needed to let this place become our tutor.

Here, in this specific place, theory would be tested against the limits and opportunities, the pressures and personalities, and the unique, real-life details that "you only know if you live here." And when my passion and preparation finally collided with the specific details of this place, my purpose clarified. The place helped teach me my purpose.

Sit in Your Cell

These are five lessons that "sitting in your cell" or staying in one place can teach you. Most of us, in our highly mobile culture, have been convinced that the answers to questions like "Who am I?" "How am I affected?" "What do I need?" "What do I want?" and "What should I do?" are discovered by going somewhere else, by moving somewhere new, by acquiring the next thing. As a result, many of us are continually searching for, but never finding, real, lasting, and fulfilling answers.

There is a connection between a person's life and a person's place—between the soul and the soil—that is often overlooked. We would do well to stick around for a while and recover it.

In November 2018 the small town of Paradise, California, was nearly completely destroyed by the most destructive forest fire in state history. Eighty-five people died. 19,000 buildings, nearly every structure in the town, were burned to the ground.

"I've got this red, Paradise dirt in my blood, in my mouth, in my nose, on my clothes . . ." said Dave Clemmons, who lost his home and all its contents in the fire. From the stoop of his dilapidated trailer parked on the side of the highway outside of Paradise, he shared this with photographer Pete Muller: "After the fire, I went to my father's house that got burned to the ground. I was standing in the driveway and I looked down at the dirt and the leaves and the twigs and I saw the dirt, the ground, that I remember as a kid. There is just something about the place. That patch of dirt. If I got on an airplane and went away for fifty years and came back to that one spot it will feel like home. I think that one little spot will always feel like home. It's indescribable."[55]

For Steve "Woody" Culleton, Paradise was the site of his rebirth from drug-addicted alcoholic to town mayor. "This town has been a place of healing and resurrection for me," he said. "Some things aren't different," he insisted, wiping tears from his eyes. "Like the sense of belonging. Even though all the visuals are different, I still belong here."[56]

There's a teaching of Jesus commonly referred to as the "parable of the soils." It includes many details about soils but really, it's about souls. It's about the battle of spiritual survival and productivity. And it speaks to the importance of stability in a place.

Here's Matthew's account:

> Then he told them many things in parables, saying: "A farmer went out to sow his seed. As he was scattering the seed, some fell along the path, and the birds came and ate it up. Some fell on rocky places, where it did not have much soil. It sprang up quickly, because the soil was shallow. But when the sun came up, the plants were scorched, and they withered because they had no root. Other seed fell among thorns, which grew up and choked the plants. Still other seed fell on good soil, where it produced a crop—a hundred, sixty or thirty times what was sown. Whoever has ears, let them hear."
> (Matthew 13:3–9)

On the surface it appears that Jesus is talking about seeds and dirt. But it's a parable—a story with a deeper meaning—so it's really not about soils. Jesus isn't talking about plants; he's talking about people. He wants his listeners not just to listen to him, but to hear what he's saying.

The constant in the story is the seed. The same seed is being sown throughout. The variable in the story is the soil—the dynamics of the place in which the seed is trying to grow. It's the variety of soils that makes the difference in the outcome.

Jesus describes what happens to seeds that fall in the four kinds of soil: Seeds on paths get snatched up by birds. Seeds in rocky places grow quickly but don't last, because the plant can't establish any roots. Seeds which land among thorns also experience initial growth, but the plants are soon choked out. They don't take root. They don't mature. Only seed that lands in good soil produces a crop. These take root, mature, and produce fruit. Good comes from this seed—not just a little good, but remarkable good. The return on the seed planted in good soil is thirty or sixty or a hundred times.

The accounts of this teaching of Jesus recorded by Mark and Luke in their Gospels include a rare explanation from Jesus about the parable:

Jesus explains that the seed represents the Word of God, and the four different kinds of soil represent four kinds of people, or, more specifically: people in four kinds of places.

Here's a portion of Luke's account:

This is the meaning of the parable: The seed is the word of God. Those along the path are the ones who hear, and then the devil comes and takes away the word from their hearts, so that they may not believe and be saved. Those on the rocky ground are the ones who receive the word with joy when they hear it, but they have no root. They believe for a while, but in the time of testing they fall away. The seed that fell among thorns stands for those who hear, but as they go on their way they are choked by life's worries, riches and pleasures, and they do not mature. But the seed on good soil stands for those with a noble and good heart, who hear the word, retain it, and by persevering produce a crop.
(Luke 8:11–15)

So according to Jesus, seeds snatched up off the path symbolize people who don't understand the Word. Seeds in rocky places which sprout quickly but don't last represent people who don't persevere. Seeds choked out by thorns picture people who don't believe the Kingdom of God is the most valuable. They're worried about and deceived by wealth and worldly priorities. Finally, the seed landing in good soil and producing an impressive crop represents people who hear, understand, and accept the truth.

The question being asked in this parable has to do with the receptivity of people to the truth of God. God's word is given to all but only takes root and produces fruit if it "lands" in a good place. What makes the place good? Any place seeds can take root, grow, and produce.

The stability of the place stands in sharp contrast to the quick and shallow and crowded nature of the other soils. It's the receptivity of the soil—or the soul—that is emphasized by Jesus.

Or, to drop some of the parable words: The stability of one person's life stands in sharp contrast to the quick and shallow and crowded nature of the other people's lives. It's the stability of a person's life which leads to production. And the essential component to that productive stability is getting rooted in this place.

Now, let me return to the story of my good friend Greg.

Once the initial shock of learning that Greg and his family were moving wore off, and I'd asked the initial questions: What did the kids say? How's Courtney? What about the church? What about the house? I finally asked, "Where are you going?"

Greg responded, "We're moving to Memphis." And the reasons why Greg and his family were moving to Memphis became clear as I spent the next few days with them in Charlottesville. Here are a few of the reasons: In Charlottesville, they knew all their neighbors. They knew who was in the hospital and who was celebrating birthdays. It was clear that they'd shared a lot of meals with a lot of these people for a lot of years. They knew the people.

Secondly, they understood the challenges and the hopes of this city. A few months prior to my visit, Charlottesville was national news because of racially charged protests that turned tragically violent. Greg understood the situation at a local level, which was in some ways not as bad as the media reported, but in most ways was actually much worse.

Greg and his family had learned the history of the place—the generational sins, institutional influences, the critical cultural and environmental contexts to so many stories—and not just from books or lectures but from people and from sharing life with them in that place. They knew the problems. They knew the brokenness. They knew it firsthand.

This leads to the third reason for their move, and it was really the critical reason: their knowledge of the city's history, challenges, and hopes extended far beyond the intellectual. They'd lived them; they'd shared in them. They'd felt and grieved and celebrated them. They had experienced this place personally. The pains of the place had affected them personally, had impacted their family. They knew how people in Charlottesville felt and what they faced because they were the people in Charlottesville. They felt that way too. They were in the same space, navigating around those same obstacles.

This long-term, localized, personalized experience in this particular place shaped their efforts to restore what was broken. And their efforts were effective because they were deeply rooted. The church which Greg led was highly effective in addressing the needs of the town because their understanding of the real issues was so clear. They knew the problems, the pain, the people, and the possibilities. For example, one morning we were walking near his office on a street in the downtown area. A FedEx truck slowed down. The driver greeted Greg by name. Greg returned the greeting, asked a specific, informed question about the man's family, and told me his story as he drove away.

Greg's eight-year-old son ran freely around the neighborhood for hours with other little boys, playing in the creek, grabbing snacks in friends' homes, as if the whole neighborhood was in on some not-yet-forgotten dream to let kids be kids and then get them home in time for dinner. Several times during my visit, Greg paused, looked over his familiar surroundings, and said quietly, "I can't believe we're leaving all this." So much of it was so good. And so much of the goodness had been established over so many years of hard work and relational commitment.

If you had walked by Greg's house in the evening, you would have seen us sitting together on the front porch drinking tea, and if you could have somehow gained a glimpse of the multifaceted success represented in that moment, you would almost certainly have thought, *That dude has made it. He's arrived. This is what so many people are trying to find. This is what so many people are trying to build. It's right here. You've found it. You've built it.*

What we all see and long for is the fruit of stability. But what very few of us, today, recognize is that this fruit cannot be bought. It is not found, it is grown. There is no shortcut to eighteen years of life and service in one city. This kind of fruit comes from deep roots. It is the fruit of stability, of having not moved for a long time.

Here's why I've told you all this about Greg. The value of stability in a specific place is why Greg and his family had stayed in Charlottesville for so long. It's because they knew that stability was the only way to experience real growth and lasting change. And the value of stability to a specific place is also why Greg and his family decided to move to Memphis.

The reason that convinced them to stay for so long was the same reason that moved them.

"We still value the same thing," he told me as we sat up late into the night on his front porch. "I believe God is calling us to move to the inner city to take this value, this commitment, and these practices—all the things we've learned *here* and live them out *there*." Their moving was not really a leaving. It was certainly not an avoiding or an abandoning or a wandering. This was movement as mission.

In staying they had gained the insights, developed the values, and lived the disciplines that would enable their moving to bring healing to another place. They were not moving to get. They were moving to give. This was not an exercise of consumerism. This was restoration in action.

They could not have learned what they knew if they had not stayed in Charlottesville for a long time. It was their stability in that place that God used to uniquely prepare them to be a stabilizing presence in another place. They were moving to Memphis. But because their movement was borne out of a long season of stability, this was movement that mattered. This movement would not perpetuate the fragmentation of family or the disintegration of communities or the hurt caused by self-obsessed consumerism. The movement would bring healing.

One More Monk Story

In Kentucky, in the middle of the twentieth century, there lived a Trappist monk named Thomas Merton. In his journal, published as *The Sign of Jonas,* Merton records his many years of wrestling with the desire to leave the Abbey of Our Lady of Gethsemani, the community of which he was a part in Kentucky. Through his frequent journal entries, he struggles almost daily with the idea that another monastery would be better than this one; another community would be better than this one; another rule of life would be better than this one. If only he could do different work, he would be more fulfilled. If only he could share life with more committed people life would be less frustrating. If only he could move to another place everything—it seemed to him—would be better.

Finally, Merton comes to a powerful realization: Echoing the famous words of Moses the Black about staying in your cell, Merton writes, "God's will is my cell."[57]

Merton knows that place matters. What he realizes is that the ultimate place he needs to be is *in God's will.* The place where he needs to stay is in God's will. It's not ultimately about Charlottesville or Memphis or Lincoln or Spain or Italy or Cambodia or Paradise. God's will is my cell. Here, in the place of full surrender to God, is where I need to stay.

Journal

Third Week at the Monastery

Something a fellow guest at the monastery says makes me realize: *Stability is motivated by love. Stability, at first, is for my sake: my formation, my heart. Later, it's for the sake of others: their formation, their hearts.*

I have a long talk—my second—with Fr. M., who is eminently kind. He begins our time together by saying, "This time is for you."

We talk about the local parish and the family (especially marriage) as critical contexts for the development of stability. He explains how worship needs liturgy: a stable form of worshiping God in spirit and in truth, through faith, reason, and adoration. Without this rootedness, our worship becomes anthropocentric, focused on feeling and sentimentalism.

He says, "Worship is not a show," and wonders aloud, "What does so much of the evangelical church have to do with Jesus?" I loved this conversation. I left feeling inspired to think and pray. And, more importantly, I left knowing that I had been shepherded.

One of the highlights of my time in Norcia was my conversation with the founding abbot of the monastery, Fr. C. It was my friend Sister Maximilian Marie's connection with Fr. C. that opened the door for my visit more than a year prior to my coming. A powerful sense of God's prevenient grace and constant goodness filled my heart as Fr. C. slowly made his way down the rock steps from the cloister to the collection of lawn chairs near the old ruins where we would spend some time talking. I took notes furiously and tried to soak up every word. Here are some of the nuggets of absolute wisdom he shared with me.

"Prayer *is* doing something. It is being still and knowing that He is God."

He likened the vow of stability to marriage. He said, "You can't run when there are problems." "When the monotony and sameness feels dull, the challenge is to go deeper." When prayer becomes routine, "You have to dig." Then prayer will "become more profound and less superficial."

In "both monastic life and married life, what is needed is sacrifice and love." People "have to see stability as desirable. Anything good requires sacrifice and a little strictness."

He feels the cultural emphasis on "self-care" is "awful and leads to unhappiness." He says, "Self-giving leads to happiness." He quotes G. K. Chesterton, who said, "Only dead things go with the current. It takes something living to go against it."

Fr. C. is sweet, thoughtful, and deeply contemplative. I could have talked to him for a long, long time, and I wish I could hear him teach. We only had thirty-five minutes, but the wisdom he shared was the fruit of years of devotion to God and the care of souls.

After Lauds, Brother B. drives me down to the center of town to catch a bus. I'm ready to go but I feel so sad about leaving. So much of my life over the last eighteen months has been focused on planning and raising money for this experience. It's hard to believe it's wrapping up. It's been three weeks since I waved goodbye to my wife and kids at the airport in Rome. I still have another five days of solitude planned. I'm missing my family. As we wait for the bus Brother B. explains how stability experienced in a person's family enables future stability, or the ability to be part of a greater whole.

It seems to me that simply being formed, early on, as part of a family creates a capacity for community that is nearly impossible to carve out after a certain age. Perhaps that's part of the reason why the monasteries I know won't even consider receiving new members once they've aged past young adulthood.

As the bus winds through the green, misty Umbrian mountains, I am gripped with emotion. I get the sense that I have tasted something of heaven. It was challenging and it was difficult. It was beautiful and it was real.

CHAPTER 5
Stability and Change
You Are the Branch

"We are the birds and you are the branch.
If you go, we lose our footing."
—OF GODS AND MEN[58]

M y confidence evaporated less than five minutes into the
hike back to camp. The strong conviction, which had
fueled months of planning, vanished into the midnight sky.
My stomach rolled and my legs forgot their strength.

Behind me, left alone in the dark, in a small tent pitched on
the edge of a cliff was my not yet thirteen-year-old son Isaiah.
Tonight was his solo: a night spent in the woods alone, the
final challenge of his rite of passage experience. As I left him
in the dark and began slowly navigating the three-quarter mile
climb back to camp, every parental instinct in my mind and
body screamed in revolt.

*"What are you thinking?" "What are you doing?" "This is a terrible
idea!"*

It wasn't the threat of physical danger that most concerned
me. It was the fear that his imagination would create monsters in
the dark, that he'd lose his nerve, become insanely frightened,

and be scarred for life. I imagined him, years later, in therapy, asking, "Why on earth would a father leave his child alone, overnight, in the woods?"

Twelve months earlier I had written letters to ten men in our community. I thanked them for being men of integrity, expressed my admiration for their solid character, and gave them a unique invitation. I asked them to support my son on a year-long journey from boyhood to young adulthood. The goal was to create a rite of passage experience that would not only help Isaiah define manhood but would also usher him into it. This would be a year of change. In order for that change to be good and healthy, it needed guidance. Their role in the process was to serve as way-markers, offering encouragement and correction and the kind of wisdom gained only through time. As a father, I was calling my son into a season of movement. I invited ten other men to contribute to the process, because this movement needed to be rooted in years of stability. Isaiah's initial movement into manhood would be rooted in the combined decades of faithfulness. This experience, I believed, would be movement that mattered.

I hardly slept on the night of my son's solo. Doubts filled my dreams. Countless scenarios played out in my mind. The minutes seemed to wander, unhurried, for hours before dawn.

Finally, the stars faded and men emerged from their tents and trucks to engage in quiet conversation around the fire. These were the ten men who had mentored my son through the previous year. They had assembled in the mountains to help articulate the values of our community and to witness and celebrate my son's transition into it. As we drank coffee and prepared breakfast, we glanced often toward the large outcropping of granite around which we expected my son's return. Then suddenly he appeared, looking peaceful and focused. As he made his way through the boulders the men stood in silence and faced him.

I dragged a line in the dirt at the edge of our campsite. My son approached the line and faced his mentors. For the next twenty-five minutes, three of them addressed him directly. They described specific elements of Christian manhood and called him to embrace and pursue them. He accepted their encouragements and readied himself for the challenges.

Finally, we invited him to cross the line. My son, the boy, stepped across. We embraced him as he joined us on the other side, in the community of men.

Why Did This Movement Matter?

Are rites of passage examples of stability or new growth? Do they celebrate long-held values or fresh potential? Are they to be understood as basic training or as wild adventures? The reason rites of passage are so powerful is that they are both/ and! Rites of passage are great examples of new movement which is full of meaning because the movement is rooted in years of stability.

I believe that there are two energies or pulls or calls in Scripture.

One is the call to stay, to remain, to abide, persevere, stand, and endure. This is the call to stability. This call is rooted in the *being* of God—the faithfulness, reliability, unchanging character of God.

The other energy or pull that shows up throughout the Bible is the call to go, to leave, to journey, pilgrimage, stretch, be united with, be transformed, venture out, cross borders, to incarnate the gospel in new places. This is the call to go. And this call is rooted in the *work* of God: the creative, restorative, God so loved the world that he sent his one and only son, engaging the brokenness, sharing meals with sinners, kicking in the gates of hell *work of God.*

We typically focus on that second call—the call to action. And, of course, this is biblical and important and needed. It's desperately needed. But this discussion about stability has been an effort to listen for and hear the first call: the quieter call. It's been an effort to consider the foundation, the roots, the bass note, that place of origin from which the building rises and the fruit blooms and the music soars and all the action comes . . . which is the place of stability.

The Bible does not pit one call against the other. It's not either/or. It's both/and. The call to go is all over the Bible— from the story of Abraham to Jesus preaching the Great Commission. But before you go, you should stay. You should not rush to go. You should stay for a while. Staying is critical to the success of your going.

Most of the time, we talk about going and doing, about the restorative work of God, the active ministry of Jesus. We rarely consider the creative power of staying.

Most of the time we talk about movement, but we have an underdeveloped understanding of the source of movement that is meaningful. We have not worked to appreciate the motive for staying.

We celebrate the harvest while underappreciating—or failing to be honest about—the years of labor. Therefore, we have little to say about staying. So, instead, we almost always talk about going.

What I'm advocating is this: in order for our movement to matter, in order for all our going and doing to make a good impact on the world, it must be different from all the busy, shallow, crowded movement happening all around us. Restorative movement is birthed from a different source. Our movement must be rooted in stability, if it is to be movement that heals the hurting.

This much is clear: The world doesn't need more talkers. The world needs people who have something good and true to say. The world doesn't need more busybodies. The world needs people who know what to do and how to do it. Yes, we need to go. The final message of Jesus to his disciples is "Go." But as with his disciples, our going must come from our being with Jesus. We need to actively and intentionally stay, so that our going is movement that matters.

Here's a teaching of Jesus that clarifies this relationship between staying and going:

The Apostle John records this near the end of Jesus's ministry. Jesus says to his disciples,

> I am the true vine, and my Father is the gardener. He cuts off every branch in me that bears no fruit, while every branch that does bear fruit he prunes so that it will be even more fruitful. You are already clean because of the word I have spoken to you. Remain in me, as I also remain in you. No branch can bear fruit by itself; it must remain in the vine. Neither can you bear fruit unless you remain in me.
>
> I am the vine; you are the branches. If you remain in me and I in you, you will bear much fruit; apart from me you can do nothing. If you do not remain in me, you are like a branch that is thrown away and withers; such branches are picked up, thrown into the fire and burned. If you remain in me and my words remain in you, ask whatever you wish, and it will be done for you. This is to my Father's glory, that you bear much fruit, showing yourselves to be my disciples. (John 15:1–8)

Notice: What is the ultimate goal of Jesus's words to his disciples? What is his desired end result? It's "that you bear much fruit."

What is the threat? What is the potential concern? What's the bad thing that might happen? The branch (which is a metaphor for you) may be "cut off."

For what reason would a branch be cut from the vine? Because it "bears no fruit."

So, bearing fruit is not just the goal, it's a requirement. It's essential. It's expected. (No wonder we focus on bearing fruit!)

And yet, what is the one thing the disciples are told to do? What is Christ's actual instruction? Jesus's clear answer, which he then reiterates for emphasis, is, "remain in me." According to the metaphorical language, the imperative is to "stay connected to the vine."

The conclusion of this teaching, which may startle those of us influenced by movement-addicted spiritual subcultures, is *staying results in being fruitful.* The normal thing for a branch to do when it remains connected to the vine is to produce much fruit. That's what happens. That's what we should expect because that's the way it's designed. Fruit is the result of sustained connection.

The only "work" the "branch"—or the person—has to do is to remain connected to the Vine, which is Jesus. We could say that Jesus's message to his disciples is, *You work on stability; I'll work on productivity.*

Churches Repairing the World

We don't need more religious museums preserving relics from a triumphant past. Some churches feel that way. We need more Christian activists engaging the brokenness, proclaiming and demonstrating truth and grace, and working to heal the wounds and the divisions that cripple us. But in order to engage in this cultural moment with wisdom, authority, and relational credibility, our activism must be deeply rooted and profoundly connected to the source of life.

Here we are! We're living in a profoundly challenging time when unprecedented, world-wide brokenness disrupts institutionalized structures and dismantles cultural assumptions. Everyone is aware of the problems. Few are offering compelling solutions.

The church need not run frantically into the chaos of the crowds. Our movement can and must be more purposeful than that. We must stay connected to the Vine so we can know what to do and have the power to do it. Our rootedness is what we bring to the table. Our stability, in a deeply destabilized world, will be our much-needed method of healing.

You and I live in a culture which wants the fruit (or the results) of stability but either refuses to recognize or simply cannot handle the means by which these results come. Our culture has largely repudiated stability. One of the things that makes stability, or remaining, unattractive is that we don't understand its posture. We don't understand what stability looks like.

For stability, we picture something that doesn't move, like a person standing still in the middle of a river, and then we mistakenly equate stability with doing nothing. But stability is not passive. Stability is active.

The posture is not sitting back and saying "whatever." It's not drifting along with the current. It's digging your toes into the river rock and leaning forward against the current and finding the grace-filled balance against the powerful forces of adversity with intentionality and purpose.

Stability is actively holding on. It's fighting to not run away when life gets hard. It's working to remain relationally connected. It's staying grounded and remaining faithful.

"Don't just stand there, do something!" is an ethic that shaped the childhood of many of us. Valuing stability sounds like the opposite of this ethic, but it's not. Stability is standing strong. It's not floating down the river on a raft, which might be a great metaphor for meaningless movement. Stability is standing against the current. Instead of "Don't just stand there, do something," our culture needs to hear, "Don't just do something, stand there!" We need to invite our busybody culture to engage in the purposeful action of stability.

Another reason stability fails to compel many of us is that we don't understand its purpose. Stability is not an end in itself. Stability is not the end goal. Stability has long been valued by the wise because of *the growth it enables*. From an historic Christian perspective, stability is the commitment to "stay," and the staying is also profoundly instrumental. It's the commitment that is made in order to accomplish some*thing* with some*one*. Without a specific community or a specific goal, the commitment to staying can seem pointless. But when I know the goal I'm working toward and I know the person or community with whom I'm working, the value of stability becomes clear. For instance, my wife and I share the common commitment to building a family with one another. The family is our some*thing*. Each of us is the other's some*one*. Stability is of ultimate importance because of the healthy family it enables.

In other words, stability says "stay" but also asks "with whom?" and "to what purpose?"[59] It's not enough for me to say, "I will stay." The specific purpose of stability is revealed when I say, "I will stay in order to pursue *this* with *you*." This is stability as Benedict envisioned it: a lifelong commitment to ongoing conversion with these people in this place.

You need to answer the "for what purpose?" question and the "with whom?" question. You need a what and a who. You need to have a clearly articulated reason.

My contention is that even though our culture admires and longs for stability's fruit, we have largely repudiated stability itself. We don't understand stability's posture—that it's active, not passive, nor do we understand its purpose—that it is unto something, that it enables something, that it is the means to an end, that committing to a specific place and a particular people and a specific way of life is all for a purpose.

Ultimately, the purpose of stability is *restoration*. Stability provides the critical context for putting broken things back together. Stability allows for real growth, strong connection, and actual fruit. Why should you stay? You should stay to work for the restoration of all things. Restoration is the church's work. Restoration is the mission.

Nevertheless, it is always innovation that gets the start-up funds. Innovation grabs the attention and woos the crowd. But it's restoration—bringing healing of the wounded and health to the hurting and wholeness to the broken—that's compelling. That is why Christ came to earth. That is the holy work of the church. Our high calling is to follow Jesus, who incarnated into culture in order to fully restore it.

Our history is marked by a range of relationships between church and culture. The church has fought to rule culture. The church has built walls to keep culture at a distance. And the church has accommodated culture so readily that all distinctions between church and culture have blurred. But Christ came to restore the world, to return all of creation to its intended purpose. Therefore, we are most faithful to our king when we engage culture with a compelling, hope-filled, restorative alternative to the destructive status quo. And to do this, we must value and practice stability.

Thomas Merton wrote, "It is pride that wants to be stripped and humbled in the grand manner, with thunder and lightning. The simplest and most effective way to sanctity is to disappear into the background of ordinary everyday routine."[60] The point of Benedictine spirituality, punctuated by the vow of stability, is that we have to decide, once and for all, what we are about and then live in a way that makes that possible and makes that real.

Consider these two very real examples.

In October 1895, eighty-two people gathered for the first meeting of a new church led by Phineas Bresee, a leading pastor in the Southern California Conference of the Methodist Episcopal Church, and Dr. J. P. Widney, a medical doctor who had served as president of the University of Southern California. Having become increasingly concerned with the plight of the urban poor, specifically families ruined by addiction to alcohol abuse, they named their community The Pentecostal Church of the Nazarene, intentionally embracing the derogatory label for Jesus. (In the gospel of John, Philip excitedly declares to his brother that they have found the Messiah in the insignificant town of Nazareth. Nathaniel's response reveals the common pejorative perspective on this unremarkable hometown: "Can anything good come out of Nazareth?") Bresee was convinced that the overlooked and undervalued "urban poor needed strong family churches in their midst to give stability to their lives and neighborhoods."[61]

They devoted the church to the twin purposes of calling the growing community to "follow Christ's example and preach the gospel to the poor."[62] They believed that a broken culture would be restored when the church put down roots and stayed put. They would not distance themselves from the segment of society most apparently corrupted by sin and sadness. They would, instead, embed themselves in the middle of it.

Stability was a key ingredient to fostering not just personal piety but "social holiness" or a religion that extended beyond the personal to the communal and even the societal.[63]

Rejecting the elegance and expensive adornment prized in houses of worship where congregants actually rented pews, and going to church was often about status, the first Church of the Nazarene plowed its resources into the work of saving souls by relieving the needs of the poor. The investment in the mission of restoring culture was made, literally, one street at a time.

Next, consider Notre-Dame de l'Atlas Monastery of Médéa, Algeria. In the introduction to this book, I briefly shared the story of the French Trappist monks who, over a period of several years in the 1990s, labored to discern whether to remain in Algeria and face near-certain, violent death or to retreat to the safety of their mother house in France. The monks' unanimous decision to stay is a remarkable example of living the vow of stability as a means of restoration.

The years of evaluation, discussion, and prayer around the possibility of leaving and the value of staying all within the context of their devotion to Jesus and their monastic vows created fertile soil for profound insights into the wisdom of stability. In the end, they decided that staying, even if staying meant dying, was the only option that provided the possibility of turning the tide of retributive violence.

Stability was critical to the mission Jesus taught his disciples in the form of a prayer, "Your Kingdom come, your will be done on earth. . . ."[64] As Jesus did, those monks had the freedom to leave. They could have escaped Algeria, and, in so doing, abandon the culture to the impending devastation of war and death. Or, as Jesus did, they could live into the fullness of the broken human condition and remain. They could face the violence. Why stay? Because they came to believe that the only way to reveal the transforming presence of the living Christ was to remain and confront brokenness with the presence of love.

Not long before he was martyred, Christian de Chergé, the abbot of the monastery, quoted the words of a friend, "We must find in the mystery of the Incarnation the true reasons for our staying here despite the threats and torment of the people. . . ." And then he added, "We, too, have to live the mystery of the Incarnation, for that is the deepest of all the reasons why we stay at Tibhirine."[65]

Christians are animated by the great hope that good things, which have become broken, will be put back together again. This is the message we carry into the world: the hope of the Resurrection culminating in the restoration of all things. In order for this truth to be experienced, it needs to be demonstrated, not just vocalized. The message must take on flesh, it must dwell among, it must "move into the neighborhood," take up residence, and remain.[66]

The enduring, stable, real-life presence of the messenger is the embodiment of the message, and that embodiment is essential.

It was not the monks' preaching which brought a sense of security to the people of Tibhirine. It was the monks' presence. Their vow of stability, faithfully fulfilled in this particular place, with these specific people, surrounded by actual dangers, was why they were valued as the "footing" of the village.

Journal
Solitude in Rome

I arrived back in Rome yesterday afternoon, where I've rented a small third-story apartment with a rooftop patio. The approximately 800 square feet of space feels extravagantly spacious after sharing a 10 x 20 storage container with up to five others over the last couple weeks.

I continue to have unusual, especially intense dreams. They are distinctly spiritual in nature and full of conflict. I was ripped out of sleep in the midst of another subconscious journey last night at 2:45 a.m. When I realized the time, I got out of bed and prayed Vigils in solidarity with my friends the monks of the Monastero di San Benedetto in Monte.

I realize now that one of the things that impressed me about the monks was how intentional they are with their movement, with their careful closing of doors, with the way they navigate the chapel and the refectory. They don't waste movement.

I hear church bells ringing all throughout Rome. In my body I feel the signal to put down my writing and walk to the chapel. Before I was even consciously aware of the sound, my soul felt stirred to move and pray.

I've been reading each of the New Testament letters in single sittings since arriving at the monastery. Powerful. The writer of Hebrews closes with "Make every effort to live in peace with all men *and to be holy.*"

The hymn at None (the 9 a.m. prayer time) says:

O Godhead, here untouched, unseen,
All things created bear your trace;
The seed of glory sown in man
Will flower when we see your face.

The personal prayer I embraced before leaving the chapel at each prayer time was this:

Christ, you are my Good Shepherd.
Speak, for your servant is listening.
Help me recognize your voice and to follow you.
Amen.

CHAPTER 6

Practices of Stability

"Miracles may show me the saint, but they do not show me how he became a saint: and that is what I want to see. . . . Tell me what was churning in his soul as he battled his way up from selfishness and the allurements of sin to the great heart of God."

—M. RAYMOND, OCSO[67]

After years of studying the vow and value of stability, I have found that one observation stands out as perhaps the most important "takeaway" from this project: True stability enables a way of being in the world that is distinctly effective. But as with a house's foundation, the value of stability may not be immediately recognized. We often don't recognize the importance of investing in and building a strong foundation.

I've been interested in houses for a long time. I've worked on construction crews and participated in restoration projects, and I enjoy talking with friends about home renovation ideas. Often, in our walks around our neighborhood, my wife and I will comment on the houses, noting creative additions and unique design choices. But in all of my conversations about houses, I have never heard anyone admire a house's foundation.

No one meets their Realtor to view a potential purchase and remarks, as they step out of their car, "Check out that foundation!" A house's "curb appeal" has more to do with the freshly painted front porch or the newly planted tulips. But none of the attractive surface details are anywhere near the value of a solid foundation. In fact, it doesn't matter how "cute" the house looks; the discovery of a faulty foundation is a deal-breaker.

We don't notice the foundation at first. But we know that it would be foolish to invest in a house built on an unstable foundation. Because life has taught us that anything built on a faulty foundation is not sound. It won't last. It's not reliable. It's all going to come crashing down.

Many, in our always-moving culture, are longing for the byproducts of stability. We want what stability provides. But the gap between what we want and where we are continues to widen for three reasons.

We do not value the commitment to stability. We deride it and diminish its importance. We prefer "tricks" and "life hacks." We search for shortcuts.

We do not consistently engage in stabilizing practices. They strike us as strange or even extreme. Regular, ongoing disciplines struggle to find their place in our lives. For instance, many of us will make the occasional financial donation, but few practice tithing. Many will try out the trending diet, but few practice regular fasting. Gym memberships are most often cancelled in March, revealing a nation-wide abandonment of well-intended New Year's plans for better health. Sadly, a night of binge-watching our favorite show on Netflix is the best example some of us can offer of an accomplishment requiring perseverance.

We do not even have language to discuss the value of stability. Our ability to articulate the psychological nuances of our purchasing preferences is impressive. We've built an arsenal of vocabulary in order to gain the advantage on the battlefield of commercialized consumerism. But we struggle to find the words needed to describe the all-too-elusive quality that illumines the fifty-year marriage or anchors the medieval prayer chapel.

So how do we do it? What are some practical ways to *do this*? Where can we begin? What are some specific first steps on this lifelong journey?

I'll offer four.

Celebrate the Root that Led to the Fruit

First, create celebrations of stability that go beyond the relatively superficial "congratulations for having endured" (twenty years of marriage, five years in the neighborhood, another year of ministry). We need to dig deeper to expose the connections between the roots and the fruit. We typically celebrate the fruit or the result of years of effort and faithfulness, but we fail to tell the full truth about the suffering, disappointment, obedience, investment, and long seasons of waiting that preceded that same fruit.

Celebrations of stability might include (perhaps counterintuitively) public goodbyes. The value we claim to place on relationships is revealed as shallow when we spend all our energy being attractive and welcoming but fail to thank and acknowledge members of our community as they move on. In the church I pastor, we will often take what some feel is an excessive amount of time or energy saying goodbye to people who are leaving our church. The common, somewhat understandable protest is, "Shouldn't we focus on those who are coming instead of those who are leaving?" What this perspective fails to realize is that when people who are considering being part of a community or who are new to a community witness the value placed on people that is demonstrated in a public goodbye, it *is* attractive. Holistic displays of a community's value of people, whether they're first-time guests or long-time members who are moving on, are stabilizing to the community.

I'm not advocating handing a microphone to everyone who leaves the church. We need to help people recognize the distinction between leaving and being sent. But the work of stability is to develop character and wisdom that can be shared. So, when healthy movement happens (leaving home for college, embarking on pilgrimage, moving to a mission field, even moving to a new city or a new church for the right reasons) it should be celebrated as the hoped-for fruit of staying in one place, sharing life with one community, or sticking with one practice for a long time.

We tend to celebrate only victories. We should also celebrate the suffering, obedience, prayers, work, waiting, and perseverance which preceded the victories. Drawing attention only to the happy ending of the story can further entrench the mistaken perspective that sees pain as pointless, suffering as unnecessary, and the decision to delay gratification as foolish. We must help people see the value in the hard parts of life. We need to celebrate the beauty of enduring through the long years between the exciting start and the victorious finish.

How will people get a vision for stability if we don't tell the full story behind the fruit we all hope to realize at some point in our lives?

Value the Permanency of People

Second, continually hold up the value of what Hubert van Zeller referred to as the "permanency of the personnel."[68] Even more important than commitment to a place is a commitment to a people—a very specific community with whom to live and learn and struggle and forgive and heal. This *relational* stability communicates deeply to the human need and longing for companionship. We must develop, nurture, and actively celebrate lasting community.

When we were gathering people in 2004 around a vision for a new church plant, I shared several ideas which I felt were compelling, but the idea that quickly gained the most traction had to do with building community. The phrase we repeated often was "We're raising our kids together." As I look back on that phrase now, it sounds a bit daunting—like an invitation to an intense, long-term commitment. But that's what some people were looking for. And that's what they bought into. We shared meals and birthdays. We cheered for one another's kids at their games. We attended lots of piano recitals and school plays. We helped one another with school field trips and doctor visits, with grocery shopping and car repairs. Really, we just shared life together. And truthfully, after several years, the phrase "raise our kids together" was rarely spoken. But last year, when our oldest, and others in her class, were preparing to spread across the country to begin their college careers, we noticed something. These kids had literally grown up in our community. Most of these kids were four or five years old when their families became part of our church. They had all been baptized here. We'd all shared in their rites of passage. Various parents had served as mentors and youth pastors and coaches.

Before my daughter left for her freshman year, she told people that the church had been a healthy source of stability for her. She talked about the confidence that had grown inside her as she shared life with at least ten or twelve adults who had "been there" and supported her as long as she could remember. Was her childhood church experience perfect? No. Of course not. But, in her words, it was "authentic." It was a safe place and a source of security. And she was filled with gratitude for this community in which life—with all its pains and joys—has happened. What she was experiencing, if you'll allow my perhaps biased diagnosis, was the effects of growing up in a culture which valued the permanency of people. She had seen people work through disagreements and stay committed to one another. She had learned firsthand that love means enduring annoyances and confronting and forgiving offenses. She had experienced a community that feels like a family and recognized that a community that feels like family is valuable. In fact, it is worth fighting for.

Develop Practices of Placement

Third, develop practices of placement that train us to resist continual, unhelpful movement and unproductive change. The ancient church offers disciplines such as silence, solitude, contemplation, and mutual confession, which are nearly forgotten today but can easily be reintroduced and taught. People today are searching for authentic contentment but don't know where to look. The church holds the key to this treasure chest of formative practices. We need to pull these practices out into the light and teach them.

Modern pilgrimages could teach us long-suffering. Limiting "mission trips" to the service of one organization or people group in one place could root our service in relationship, that is, in a mutual receiving rather than a one-way handout of religious goods. Shared rituals, such as common meals and prayers (rather than a never-ending diet of new and better), must become core to the church's programming.

Community and family traditions, such as rites of passage, shared celebrations, and common benedictions anchor people to a place. They help develop a sense of familiarity and belonging. Returning to the same pool at the same park for the same barbeque lunch and the same field games played by the same fathers and sons every summer, year after year, until the sons become fathers, is stabilizing. These are the simple parts of life: playing, eating, worshiping, celebrating, that root us to a people and a place.

Practices of placement are like three-generation pictures. Have you seen them? There's a picture of a gray-haired guy in his sixties standing next to a guy who looks like a younger version of himself holding a baby. Or maybe it's a baby, with her mother, who is with *her* mother. These multigenerational pictures are images of who we are and who we are becoming. They communicate belonging and responsibility in the same instant. This is what practices of placement do. They guide our becoming. And they reveal our values to the next generation.

Practices of placement are the "nuts and bolts" of a culture. "This is what we do," we say with passion, because what we really mean is "this is who we are."

Family—the Primary Community

Fourth, we need to redouble our efforts to support family as the primary formational community. The monastery, the church, and even athletic teams can become healthy, stable, powerfully transformational communities—but they are all, in one sense, just trying to be "like a family." Nearly everyone I talked to over several years of researching the value of Christian stability ended up talking about the family. The family is unrivaled in its potential to be the physical presence of stability.

The church can support the family, and in some ways, the church can *become* a family, but it is almost impossible to overstate the importance of family itself—what some call the "domestic church." Home is where we learn to trust or distrust. Family is where we are first shaped by the loving presence—or the tragic absence—of the parent. Simply stated, the family is where real life happens.

Churches should advocate for family cohesion by balancing age-specific formation classes with full-family worship gatherings. Most of our culture works to disintegrate the family. The church community should be a multigenerational experience that truly strengthens—and doesn't compete with—the family. This is not to say that we should always defer to the family or that the family shouldn't sacrificially serve the church. (Family can become an idol like anything else.) I'm simply acknowledging that for those of us who are not committed to a traditional monastic life, the bulk of our formation will come from our family, not the church. And the place where our influence will be the most deeply felt will be the family, not the church. Therefore, the church should equip individuals to "work out their salvation" within the context of a family structure. If the gospel doesn't work *where we live*, in our homes, then we need to work to apply the gospel more practically. Similarly, if the family is not equipped and supported by the church to be a place of spiritual formation, then the church is missing its most promising method of passing the story of God's love and grace from one generation to the next.

With remarkably better rates of success than any other method I've uncovered, stable families raise people who build stable churches which become the stabilizing presence of love in our neighborhoods, our nation, and our world.

CHAPTER 7

Where Do We Stay from Here?

"Should I stay
or should I go now?"

—THE CLASH, 1982

We rooted this stability discussion in the nature of God: the faithful, reliable, always here, stable presence of God. Then, in light of God's presence, we considered our restlessness and the common human tendency to run. Next, we applied the wisdom of stability to our relationships with people and with place. And then we considered the impact of the decisions of some to stay and asked, "Could embracing stability be an effective method of healing a broken world?" Finally, I suggested several stabilizing practices—or actions— for families and communities in order to become a stabilizing presence in an increasingly destabilized world.

In this final chapter, I'll offer guidance for where to go from here.

As a pastor I am frequently asked to help discern whether an individual should stay or go. Should she stay home and attend the local junior college or move away for school?

Should he stay with the company or venture out to start his own? Should they stick with the original plan or is it time to try something different? Should they try to salvage the devastated relationship or is it best to move on? It's in navigating these practical, real-life challenges that I've labored to discover the way of stability.

We typically see just two options: stay or go. Stick with the old or explore something new. But this journey into embracing a Benedict-inspired life of stability has revealed to me a beautiful, albeit challenging, third option: I could *get closer.*

I could get closer to the root of the issue.

I could press deeper into the core of the question.

I could lean into the source of life, the real need, the true passion.

The options are not just stay or go. There is also *closer.* Valuing stability is embracing the invitation to move *closer to the root.* The way a monk does.

The Monastery, the Church, and the Culture

The life of a monk is easily dismissed as extreme. We may wonder, what good are monks accomplishing? Or how are they relevant to real life? Because their way of living is so uncommon.

To be precise, monks are not extremists, they are radicals. A radical (from the Latin, *radix*) is one who lives close to the root or the source. By contrast, an extremist is one living on the outer edge, at the farthest distance from the center. If God is the source of life, then living life with the singular focus of total devotion to God, or *monastic life,* is living close to the root, not far from it. Monastic life is radical, not extreme. The life of the monk is a remarkably unified and focused effort to draw closer to God.

Seeing things through this lens of closeness—or proximity—to the source illuminates the rarely understood relationship between the monastery, the local church, and the broader culture.

Simply stated, the monastery is called to be for the local church what the local church is called to be for the city that surrounds it. The monastery is meant to be a radical (not extreme) reference point for the church, a physical demonstration of life lived close to the root. Monks, in their radical way of living, model devotion to God not as a part of life, but as the essence of it. Modern non-monastic Christians can learn from monks how to get closer to God.

In a similar way, a city should be able to look to the local church as "the light of the world" pointing the broader culture to the true source of life (Matthew 5:14). The people in our neighborhoods ought to be able to witness the local church community compellingly revealing the way to life with God.

When the church loses its way, loosens its commitment to social holiness, and abandons its witness to the people of the city, it's the monastery—those pursuing radical closeness to the source—that reminds the church of its God-given purpose.

Throughout history, it has been the monastery that has called the church to spiritual attentiveness and devotion. The monastery has demonstrated for the church how to live in intentional committed community. The monastery has been the stabilizing force in crumbling societies, providing medical care, cultivating the land for the production of crops, catalyzing small businesses. The monastery has remained. During the fifth and sixth centuries, when Rome fell and was pillaged by the Vandals, and then by the Goths, and then by the Visigoths, and then by the Huns . . . Benedictine monasteries endured and persevered as a beacon of stability amidst the chaos and destruction.

Years ago, while I was discussing with my spiritual director my efforts to restore my own town, he kept pointing me to monks as role models. *Monks as models for cultural restoration?* He said, "Without monasteries Western civilization would have been lost. And without monks today, civilization won't be saved. It will spiral again into chaos." What I've come to understand is that in the absence of true radicals—that is, those consistently moving closer to the root—society runs faster and farther away from the source of life until it occupies only the outer extremes. Only a stable, well-ordered life, which whether "staying" or "going" is pressing ever closer to God, will keep us from careening over the edge into destruction. We need real life examples who will authentically offer compelling, life-giving alternatives to the destruction of self-centered consumerism. And some of the most inspiring, culture-shaping "influencers" I've encountered are living within the walls of monasteries.

During the time I spent with monks, I was most intensely challenged by their practice of prayer. Monks pray a lot. They pray all throughout the day.

Praying throughout the day has been a consistent element of worship all the way back to the Old Testament. For instance, in Psalm 119:164, King David writes, "Seven times a day I praise you for your righteous laws." These times of prayer were probably not seven random times. David was likely following a structured schedule of "praying the hours." We see the faithful still doing this in the New Testament. There are quick references to the practice in the background of the stories, such as in Acts 3:1: "One day Peter and John were going up to the temple at the time of prayer—at three in the afternoon." The original language there actually says, "at the ninth hour"—meaning the ninth hour of daylight. This was not just a random time when Peter and John felt like praying and the place of prayer was open; this was *the* time, or one of the times, of prayer. And it still is: it's called None—Latin for "ninth."

So, praying at set times throughout the day is not something monks invented; it's something that has been part of Christianity since the very beginning.

The monks I lived with absolutely still pray like this. The bell for the first prayer time of the day rang every morning at 3:15 a.m. The bell continued to call the monks to put down their tools and gather for prayer every few hours after that until sunset. From the start of the day to the finish, Benedictine monks devote about eight hours every day to prayer.

During my stay at the monastery, I felt as if I prayed all day long. Actually, it was more than a feeling. I literally prayed more in one day at the monastery than I typically do in a week at home. When I began sharing with friends at home about the monk's commitment to frequent, regular prayer, more than one commented, "Sounds extreme." Some revealed a commonly held perspective on the futility of prayer by wondering, "How do they get anything done?" Or "What good does that accomplish?" I also heard, "But what's the value in praying by rote? It sounds mechanical, not meaningful."

Is seeing prayer as the primary work of the day an extreme position? Is praying multiple hours before breakfast a royal waste of time?[69] Is devoting a significant portion of the day to communing with one's Creator and Redeemer somehow futile? Or does the monk's remarkable practice of prayer call one back to what matters most? Does this radical practice remind a person of their true source of life?

In fact, living with monks revealed my own extreme perspective on prayer. I felt as if I wasn't accomplishing anything. I wasn't getting enough done. I was "just praying" all day. It's clear, when I look at how little time I typically spend praying—especially compared to the time I spend working—which activity I believe to be most valuable, which activity I believe to be "accomplishing something." But this perspective is actually extreme.

It may not appear to you that way. You may see praying for ten minutes a day and working for ten hours a day as normal . . . just real life. I wonder, is it the people who pray all day or the people who rarely pray who are the real extremists? Which ones are out on the edge? Which ones are far from the source of life?

Can you imagine spending most of a Saturday with a beloved family member or friend and at the end of the day hearing them say, "Well, we hiked and talked for hours but, you know, we really didn't accomplish anything"? Do you think that might be a sign that their perspective on the day is a bit off? . . . out on the outer edge? . . . a bit extreme? If a day at the beach with your child is perceived to be a waste of time because nothing of significance was completed, perhaps you're missing the point of a day at the beach.

Maybe we need to get a bit closer to the root. Perhaps we need to become a bit more radical with our understanding and practice of prayer. I know I do.

King David prays, "I do not concern myself with great matters or things too wonderful for me. But I have calmed and quieted myself, I am like a weaned child with its mother; like a weaned child I am content."[70] In other words, David is content to just be with God . . . like a weaned child who doesn't need to nurse, isn't asking for anything from the mother, isn't drawing from her, but is content to just be with her. Being with her is all the child wants to "accomplish."

I asked one of young monks about the fact that they spend so much time praying. His response surprised me a bit. He

said, "The only work that matters is the work we do for God."[71]
That was such a great answer! He didn't say, "The work most
people do doesn't matter." Nor did he say, "Prayer is all that
matters." He said praying is work that matters—it has value—
because we do it for God.

Living with monks reminded me of the radical value of
prayer. Living with monks also reminded me of the radical
purpose of prayer. After just a few days at the monastery, I had
prayed for everything and everyone I could think of. Then that
bell would start ringing again. . . . It'd be time to pray again
and I'd wonder, *What am I going to pray for now?*

There was another challenge that I haven't yet mentioned:
most of the prayers we were praying in the monastery were
right out of the Psalms, so there was lots of confession of sin,
lots of honest and raw expression of emotion, and lots of
adoration of God. I was firmly confronted with the reality that
I simply don't do much of any of that: not much confession,
very little emotion, and almost no adoration.

I mostly just talk to God about people and tasks. My prayer
primarily centers around what I have to do and who I need to
take care of. I realized I had embraced an extreme purpose of
prayer, one that was neither biblical nor healthy. Because my
relationship with God in recent years has mostly focused on
figuring out what to do and then getting that stuff done, my
prayer practice has felt like a business agreement.

The tragic reality of many marriages is that they have lost
relational intimacy. That relational connection that goes
beyond business, beyond shared responsibility of children, is
essential to a fulfilling union. The same is true for a person's
relationship with God. My point is not that one needs to "feel
close" to God. Feelings come and go. At the monastery I was
confronted with the reality that God should be worshiped,
praised, and adored, and my relationship with God had not

included much of that. It had been on the extreme end of relationship, almost as if God were a venture capitalist and I was the founder of a start-up. I was interacting with God as if I were working with his money trying to do something worthwhile.

After about a week of praying, when this realization became clear, I stopped asking for direction and clarity and help with my tasks. Instead, I prayed for grace to match my heart to the words of psalms. I joined in the adoration of God. Then I'd come back an hour later and adore him again . . . and then again . . . and again. Slowly, the process of putting down my work and walking to the chapel became less about me and more about God.

Did I need to ask him for the same thing I asked him for two hours ago? No. There was no need for that. Did I need to thank him for his goodness, sing of his faithfulness, worship him as my God and King? Yes. There was, and is, plenty of room in my life for lots more of that.

The Real Work of God

In the *Rule*, St. Benedict writes, "Nothing is to be preferred to the Work of God."[72] And by "work of God" Benedict means prayer.

During the first week at the monastery, I felt as if the monks were always taking breaks from the work they were doing so that they could pray. After about a week I realized that the work they were doing was prayer. Occasionally they would take breaks from praying to do anything else. Finally, the monks pointed me to a radical perspective on prayer. It was prayer that was the reference point throughout the day. Everything happened either before or after prayer. Rarely did anyone say, "Meet at the truck at 7 a.m." They'd say, "Meet at the truck after Lauds." Dinner wasn't at 7 p.m., it was after Vespers.

This prayer-as-reference perspective communicated the powerful root message about prayer: all of life comes from God. Without saying it explicitly, but simply through the demonstration of a radical commitment to praying, the monks were reminding me, their town, and all who come into contact with them that all of life comes from God. Peace comes from God. Wisdom's source is God. Communing with God is the root of life. Everything emanates from God. Prayer is not an optional add-on. It's not supplemental. It is essential. Our connection with God is the reference point, not something we try to fit into our schedule or do "real quick" before the main event.

In the book of Nehemiah, we find this beautiful scene when the people of God return to rebuild the temple and their homes in Israel after generations of captivity in Babylon. A community-wide celebration is held when the holy Scriptures, which were lost, are found.

For a quarter of the day—three hours—the whole nation stands and reads the words of the law of God. For the next three hours they confess their sins and worship the Lord.

The song they sing begins like this:

Blessed be your glorious name, and
may it be exalted above all blessing and praise.
You alone are the LORD.
You made the heavens, even the highest heavens,
and all their starry host, the earth and all that is on it,
the seas and all that is in them.
    You give life to everything,
    and the multitudes of heaven worship you.
(Nehemiah 9:5–6)

"You give life to everything" is the truth they sing. And their response to that truth is, "We're turning to you. . . ." They're declaring, "You, God, are the reference point." Our life is a gift from God. Our breath is a gift from God. All that I am and all that I have comes from God.

Too often I try to "fit prayer into my busy life." That's a common approach to prayer in our culture. But it's an extreme approach to prayer—it's way out on the outer edge. It's an approach to prayer that treats the source of life as though it were an optional condiment.

Radicals, such as monks, those who live close to the root of life, show me the direction I need to move. I need to move closer to God. They remind me that at all times and in all ways, God is the source of life. Whether I'm "staying" or "going," the invitation is to move closer to God.

Comfort is Overrated

In addition to showing us the values and practices we need to move toward, radicals reveal the values and practices we need to leave behind. Cultural norms are exposed as extremely out of tune. Discovering how fully we've bought into these cherished societal values can be jarring, disorienting, and downright irritating.

What's remarkable about radicals is they don't have to say anything to point us to the root or the source of life. They just show us. Do you know how many sermons I heard while living for nearly three weeks at the monastery? Zero. No one preached to me. I just lived with these monks. And just seeing the way they live was remarkably effective in exposing my cultural values.

If the way a person prays reveals something core about their relationship with God, the way a person eats likely says a lot about a person's preferences and cultural perspectives. Cultural norms typically have to do with the basic elements of life, like food.

The practices I'm discussing here are praying and eating. But ultimately these practices are connected to something much deeper. I'll get to that. First let me tell you how hungry I was. In a typical day at home, I might pray and read for about thirty minutes before I eat. In a normal day at the monastery, I'd participate in six prayer gatherings and two reading sessions over a ten-hour period before the first meal. That was tough.

On normal days the monks would eat two meals: at 1pm and at 7pm. On "fasting days" they would eat just one meal at 5pm. They observed two to four fasting days each week.

One of the basic challenges of my time at the monastery was that I was constantly hungry. I went from three weeks of vacationing with my family during which we ate all day long—I think we enjoyed gelato thirty-one times in thirty days—to eating relatively sparingly at the monastery. At home in California, my wife shared with a family member, "Nate's having a hard time. He's constantly hungry." To which they responded, "Why doesn't he just walk to town and buy some food?" Then Matthias, my eight-year-old, chirped from the back seat, "Maybe he just wants to embrace their lifestyle."

He was right.

I'd been reading about Benedictine monks for almost a decade. So, I knew a few things about monks, but nearly everything I knew I'd learned from books. Now I wanted to go and live with them and, yes, even if just for a few weeks, embrace their lifestyle as best as I could.

The question I was most asked upon my return was, "What was that like?" It was uncomfortable. It was physically challenging. But what was even more challenging than being hungry was how violently my body, my mind, and my soul rebelled against the discomfort. My reaction to the mild-yet-prolonged discomfort was illuminating. I was convicted by just how committed I am to being comfortable.

I think of myself as a person who is focused on serving the needs of others. But I was disappointed at how self-consumed I became when my basic human appetites were not being consistently satisfied. I do OK loving God and loving others when I'm comfortable, rested, and well-fed. But remove a couple meals . . . and apparently that's all it takes turn my focus from others back to myself. Subtract a couple thousand calories and I'm struggling.

Why was this surprising? First, I've read the Bible. Is there a single faithful character in Scripture who doesn't experience significant discomfort, if not full-blown suffering? No. There's not. And I know that.

Moses wanders forty years in the desert while being constantly criticized. King David is perpetually surrounded by enemies. Paul is shipwrecked and beaten and often hungry. Jesus is tempted, plotted against, homeless, betrayed, and finally murdered. It's actually hard to imagine anyone going into a cave, reading the Bible, and emerging with the proclamation, "Serving God is easy! Here are three simple steps to a comfort-filled life." It's remarkable that we expect—and even feel entitled to—a certain level of comfort, as people whose spirituality is informed by the Holy Bible. A spirituality that values creature comforts has no home in this book.

Any yet there are a lot of "Christian" voices talking about financial prosperity. There's a surge of emphasis on self-care. There's remarkable pressure on church leaders to make church not just accessible, but "easy." I've been in Northern

California churches where someone from the platform has literally said, "We just want you to sit back, relax, and enjoy the service." I wonder, "How do you reconcile this premium on personal comfort with the teachings of Jesus?" Yet I also experience this very same tension within myself. When I'm feeling hungry, that self-focused voice inside gets really loud. Like a toddler, it demands to be satisfied.

A second reason I was shaken by just how difficult it was to feel physically uncomfortable is that I was there to grow. I expected a certain level of difficulty. I wanted a challenge. Can you think of any kind of personal growth or professional development or new birth or improvement in health that makes personal comfort a top priority? I can't. Comfort is not a priority when you are working out. In fact, it's not even a value. No one expects to feel comfortable while they're doing sit-ups. Sometimes, workout plans call for a person to do a certain exercise "to the point of exhaustion." Pushing your body until you physically can't do it anymore is not a comfortable experience, nor is it meant to be. Why? Because that point between comfort and discomfort . . . that's when new growth happens!

Many of us will willingly follow fitness coaching that pushes us to, and beyond, points of comfort. Many of us will willingly follow educational or professional guidance that pushes us to, and beyond, points of comfort. But somehow, we expect to develop a spirituality powerful enough to make a real difference in life without breaking a sweat, while maintaining a high premium on personal comfort. How does that make any sense? It's naive to think you could grow your business, your body, or your soul with a perspective that says, "I'll do it as long as I'm comfortable." Sometimes, when our faith gets difficult, we can think, "What's wrong?" Maybe nothing's wrong. Maybe the difficulty is just a good part of the process.

Who would actually believe that the best way to grow in wisdom and strength is to prioritize personal comfort? I don't think any of us would believe that. But as soon as our stomach starts growling, we think, "Man, I'm starving. I need some chips." And our desire for comfort crowds out our desire for spiritual growth. Most of the time, we want to be more comfortable more than we want to be more powerful. Are physical comfort and spiritual growth always in conflict? Not always. But often. Are personal comfort and spiritual growth mutually exclusive? No, but the desire for comfort is often the biggest practical roadblock to spiritual growth.

The challenges I faced through the basic spiritual disciplines of prayer and fasting are not ultimately about prayer or fasting. The challenges expose a deeper question which resides at the core of my life and addresses so many of the practical issues in my life. Am I pursuing greater comfort or greater devotion? What kind of life am I pursuing? What does my calendar reveal? What story do my credit card statements tell? These are simple but challenging questions. Greater comfort and greater devotion are not necessarily in conflict, but they often are.

"Comfort is complicated," said Brother A., as we waited for the occasional visitor to the monastery's temporary beer shop.

"Yes it is," I agreed, my stomach growling.

Then the bell rang again, and we headed off to prayer. . . .

Guidance and Spiritual Discernment

The wisdom of stability applies to every part of our lives. It informs our understanding of God and of ourselves, strengthens relationships, gives meaning to location, and clarifies purpose. Often this wisdom is barely noticeable. It's running in the background. We may not even be conscious of whether or not it's informing our decisions. But eventually, everyone faces the choice that most directly taps into the wisdom of stability, namely, should I stay or should I go?

The wisdom of stability offers no hard and fast rules. But it should be seriously consulted. The beautiful reality is that you can discern what God wants you to do. Of course, it's not a formula and it cannot be forced. But we're thousands of years into a tradition of people like you and me who discern the will of God through God's Word, God's Spirit, and God's community. We can read the Word of God—we live in a time and place in history with unrivaled access to the Bible. We can receive the guidance of the Holy Spirit— I'm talking about the mystical, often intangible sense of spiritual direction. We can wrestle through our questions with others, gaining their perspectives, their advice, their counsel.

It might be helpful to imagine this visually. Let's sketch two pictures.

A House

The house represents community. Your church. Your family. This is the day-to-day context of life in which the questions of life happen. House equals community. Spiritual discernment happens in this place with these people.

The house (community) is built on a foundation. That foundation is truth. It's tradition. It's the source of authority. From the Christian perspective, the foundation is the Word of God. Spiritual discernment is informed by this truth.

And surrounding the house (community) which is built on a foundation (truth) is an energetic force which affects everything. I've symbolized this here as the sun. This force/power is the real presence of God's Spirit. Spiritual discernment happens under the guidance of the Holy Spirit, which, Jesus says, "blows wherever it pleases" (John 3:8).

This picture of a house built on a rock is actually one of the more familiar metaphors for life used by Jesus. Both Matthew and Luke record Jesus teaching that those who hear his words and put them into practice are like a wise man who built his house on the rock. To be clear, Jesus's point is the "putting his teachings into practice" part. But the picture creates this memorable visual of stability and confidence even in the midst of life's storms. Whether God is calling you to stay or to go, the reality is that *you can know*. You can know the will of God.

There are some basic requirements related to Word, Spirit, and Community.

First, the basic belief that the Bible is God's Word and, as such, carries uncommon authority. You should ground your life in God's Word. To a significant degree, God's will for your life has been made known in the pages of the Bible.

Second, an openness to the guidance of the Holy Spirit. You need to believe that God is personally interested in your life and be open to his specific guidance—not just the general

"Thou shall not steal" guidance or the "Love God, Love Neighbor" guidance, but the more unique-to-you guidance: Apply for this job. Call this person. Don't say anything right now, just pray. . . .

Third, a commitment to community. You're not trying to figure out God's will for your life in isolation, all by yourself. We've all got blind spots. Even our own desires can deceive us. We need others to help us discern God's will. This is not an option. This is a basic requirement.

There are several examples in Scripture of seeking counsel from the community. One really interesting scene in Acts is when the Jesus movement extends beyond the Jewish community, non-Jewish people start to follow Jesus, and the big question becomes, "Do the non-Jewish Christians have to do all the Jewish stuff?" In response to this question the church studies and prays and talks and finally they say, "It seemed good to the Holy Spirit and to us . . ." (Acts 15:28). They deliver their conclusion.

Belief in the Bible. Openness to the Holy Spirit. Commitment to community.

A second picture is based on the teachings of John Wesley, a missionary from England to the "New World" in the 1700s who ends up starting the Methodist Church which, by 1900, becomes the biggest church in America. He taught about spiritual discernment—about knowing the will of God—and his early students organized his teachings on the topic in the shape of a quadrilateral:

The base of the quadrilateral is the Word. This is the foundation. The Word carries a disproportionately significant authority. (It's the Wesleyan quadrilateral, not the Wesleyan square). One of the sides of the quadrilateral represents Tradition/Community (church community and historic church). The other side represents Experience: the mystical sense of call, the perception of God's direction, the experience with the Holy Spirit.

So far, this picture includes the same three elements as the house diagram. But to the house diagram, Wesley explicitly adds *reason*. His addition of reason perhaps reflects a shift from the worldview of the Middle Ages, which said, *It's true because the Church says it's true*, to the modernist world view which says, *It's true because it makes sense to me*.

One hundred years before Wesley, the philosopher René Descartes wrote, "I think, therefore I am." Independent thought found its place at the table. One of the ramifications was the growing conviction that a person need not check their brain at the door of the church. We can use reason/rational thinking as a legitimate part of discerning the will of God. Wesley is careful to emphasize the authority of the Word in this whole process. If tradition doesn't jibe with the Word, if my experience doesn't resonate with the Word, if my reason contradicts the Word . . . I should submit to the Word of God.

What I find so interesting about this is that 300 or so years ago, Wesley was arguing for the inclusion of reason in spiritual discernment. But today, after 300 years of modernism and the enlightenment and the industrial revolution and the scientific method, we've made discernment all about reason.

Typically, we're trying to figure out the right answer to questions like "should I stay or should I go" without relying on the Holy Spirit and without the spiritual tradition of the Word and the church. Which leaves us with only reason.

If discernment is all about reason, then my focus becomes acquiring more and better information, not drawing closer to the source of my life through spiritual disciplines such as prayer and fasting. If all we have is reason, then discernment is as simple as a piece of paper with a line down the middle of it. One side is pros. One side is cons. Give each pro and each con a numerical value, add up each side, compare the sums, and there's your answer. If the decision is purely rational, then you don't need God's guidance, the wisdom of the historic faith, or a personal sense of calling. But the decision is probably not purely rational. And you'd probably really appreciate a sense of divine guidance in that decision you're trying to make right now, if that's actually possible.

God does guide people, and people can know his will. Spiritual discernment is a reality that we read about all throughout the Bible and the history of the church. In other words, we have a body of knowledge that includes actual wisdom about discerning the will of God for our lives.

The problem is, we've been taught to be incredibly skeptical of the supernatural. So, we're mostly clueless about a relationship with the Holy Spirit. And we've become incredibly skeptical of religious organizations. So, we're mostly wandering around in the dark without the wisdom of the Christian tradition. As a result, most of us, and I would include myself in this group, are relatively unskilled at discerning God's direction . . . especially compared to the prophets and apostles and early leaders of the church whom we read about in the Bible. But we can grow in this area of knowledge, and we really *need* to grow in this ability to draw closer to the heart of God. Because we're always being confronted with challenging situations which require us to make decisions . . . including various versions of the decision to "stay" or to "go."

Good Reasons to Stay or Go

Understanding that this question can be—and should be for the Christian—viewed within the context of spiritual discernment, here are some good reasons to stay and some good reasons not to stay, from a Biblical perspective.

A good reason to stay or go is a call from God. This is the most common good reason for staying or for going in the Bible: responding in obedience to whatever "God said." In the Old Testament, God's call comes through prophets and angels (or messengers). In the New Testament, God's call comes through angels (such as Gabriel's announcement to Mary), through God's son, Jesus, and, later, through Jesus's apostles, who reveal very practical instruction such as who should stay to serve the widows and who should go travel with Paul as he plants churches.

Not everyone can testify to having experienced a specific sense of divine direction. Such experiences are inherently subjective and can be misunderstood or mistakenly attributed to God. But when a person believes they have been called by God, the depth of confidence beneath their decision is profound. One good and long-held reason to stay or to go is a "call from God."

A second good reason to stay or go is a personal passion, or burden, or an unusual sense of care for something. St. Paul refers to a fascinating scene in his letter to the Galatians in which the fellowship of the apostles discerns that Paul should go preach to the Gentiles—the non-Jews—and Peter should stay and preach to the Jews (Galatians 2:7–9). Paul seems to have a passion, or a burden, or perhaps even an unusual ability to care for non-Jews.

I think some of the good that can come out of all the emphasis in our culture on knowing yourself well—identifying your Top Five Strengths or your Myers-Briggs results or what number you are on the Enneagram—is that if we can understand what really fires us up, what we're really passionate about, or, on the shadow side, what makes us angry, this can help us clearly identify our passion.

A good reason to stay or to go is to work and serve and live in the area of your greatest passion, especially when that passion corresponds to another good reason to stay or go, which is need.

We're so overwhelmed with the needs in our world that we underestimate the legitimacy of responding to a need as a good reason to stay or go. Certainly, the words of the prophets and of Jesus emphasize the importance of responding to a need. In other words, if someone is hungry, we should go feed them (whether we feel passionate about it or not). If someone is grieving, we should stay home and grieve with them (whether that's our gift or not). Need is almost always a good reason to stay or go.

A fourth good reason to stay or to go is abuse. It's possible to be manipulated by a person's, or a situation's, neediness. People can be abusive. Situations can be toxic.

I asked a friend of mine how he was so sure leaving this great job was the right decision. He answered without hesitation, "The environment was toxic." At first, I was skeptical. Was this just a fancy way of saying, "I didn't like it there"? Later he explained there was significant drug use among his colleagues, and he had struggled with this same thing in the past. He needed to go. Staying, in that situation, for him, was not a good decision. The destructive, abusive situation was a good reason to go.

One of my concerns whenever I teach about leaning into the pain or enduring suffering or sticking with it or facing your fears is that someone in an abusive relationship will hear me and think they should stay in the relationship. I don't ever mean that. Abuse is a good reason to leave. Protecting yourself from further abuse and/or another destructive situation down the road is a good reason to leave.

Not Good Reasons to Stay or Go

There are also not-so-good reasons to stay or go.

In most cases, fear is not a healthy motivator. When I find myself hesitating to do the hard thing—putting off the phone call, rescheduling the difficult conversation—it's usually because I'm afraid. I should always push through that because the Christian should not be motivated by fear. When I feel God's call or a burden to help someone in need, but I hesitate because I'm afraid of what it will end up costing me in time or money, that's just fear and it's not a good reason.

We're told over and over and over again in the Bible, "You don't have to be afraid." And the one reason we're given is "Because God is with you." So it's okay to say, "I'm afraid to stay." Or "I'm afraid to go." But I shouldn't allow that fear to be my reason for staying or going, because either way, God is with me.

A second not-so-good reason to stay or go is conflict. We're in a culture where conflict happens often, and we're mostly taught to avoid it. The most common reason people leave a community is they are in conflict with another person. Conflict is not a good reason to go.

In Matthew 18 Jesus himself lays out a four-part plan for *working through* conflict. Conflict is an opportunity to grow. It's a chance to extend and receive grace. It's not a good reason to stay or go. Life becomes smaller and smaller if you allow "avoiding conflict" to be your reason for what you do.

Sometimes conflict or pain or frustration lasts for a long time—for a season. This can wear down our resolve. This can erode our sense of calling. This can cause us to ignore legitimate needs. But "bad seasons" are bad reasons to stay or to go. I've noticed that quite a few people who leave because of a "bad season" step right into another "bad season" the next place they go. If you never hang in there through a bad season at work, or work through a bad season of marriage, there is a whole real-life skill set you'll never develop.

We prefer instant solutions. This tendency sometimes turns us into people who have an inability to stick with a challenge long enough to see broken things get restored.

When a person confesses to me, "I'm in a really bad season," I become interested in the conversation. Because now I have questions. What are you learning? What's broken? What needs to change? What is this bad season revealing to you about your needs? Where's God in this bad season? But all of that gets tossed out if the person has already decided, "We're in a really bad season, so we're out."

That's not a good reason. You are arresting your own development. You are short-circuiting your own growth. Most—if not all—of your truly valuable insights about life will come right near the end of bad seasons. Don't leave because you're in a bad season.

Years ago, at the outset of my study of Benedict's Rule, I understood stability to be a value that would primarily shape my relationship with place and probably also affect my relationships with people. But increasingly I'm realizing, with wonder, how valuing stability is transforming every aspect of my life.

For some, valuing stability might mean committing to a plan. Rather than constantly changing lanes in your business strategy or trying out the newest fashion or workout or parenting trends, embracing stability means finding a good plan and sticking with it. For many the call to stability invites a far more intentional commitment to a specific community. Rather than daily evaluating others, stability translates to focusing on serving others, being there for others, becoming the source of consistency and security for others. For others, the call to stability boils down to a commitment to persevere. Embracing stability means not giving up. Stability is the commitment to finish strong. There's no single application of the value and practice of stability. Choosing stability could mean finishing an hour of prayer, following through on a challenging, multi-year project, pressing deeper into marriage through changing stages of life, or devoting decades of investment to a single neighborhood.

I'm challenged in all of these ways. The primal impulse to run still whispers to my soul, especially when so much of the world seems to crumble further into chaos. In the face of destabilizing change, Benedict's radical solution compels me to dig deeper, to draw closer to the true source of life.

My hope is that this conversation has helped to open your eyes to the personal and social erosion caused by our culture's constant movement and alarming willingness to opt for the next or the new. I hope you're realizing that this hypermobile way of living has no roots and produces no fruit.

I hope you're seeing the emptiness of the cultural norm of constant change and the comparative value and worth and wisdom of stability. I hope that you're seeing that the decision to grow in stability is worth it. I hope you're recognizing stability as a powerful force for healthy change. I hope that as you consider the growing complexities of broader cultural and spiritual issues, you'll begin by embracing the value of stability as an essential ingredient of wholeness.

And I hope you'll believe that the change we seek begins right here, right now, and that you'll join me and others in doing the difficult work needed to restore all things. May you draw close to God, the giver of life. May you remain in the Vine that is Christ. And may you become the branch that provides much-needed footing in this world of constant change.

Stability Diagram

A good image is so helpful, so clarifying—such as the picture of stability from the Psalms: a large and healthy oak tree, roots sinking deep and branches reaching wide. Diagrams can be similarly helpful, if they're able to communicate complex ideas on a single page. Here's a brief explanation of the following (somewhat clumsy) diagram of the core content of this book.

I share the view articulated by others that St. Benedict's key contribution to monastic life, and ultimately, to the Church, is the value and vow of stability. I argue that the core frustration addressed by Benedict in his Rule is consumerism. So, essentially, I am contrasting the (relatively rarely held) value of stability against the (widely embraced) value of consumerism.

Most importantly, the diagram contrasts the quality of movement that comes from living the value of stability against the movement that comes from living the value of consumerism. Movement "birthed" from stability is meaningful. It ultimately restores all things. Movement "birthed" from consumerism is destructive. It ultimately abandons all things.

Stability Diagram

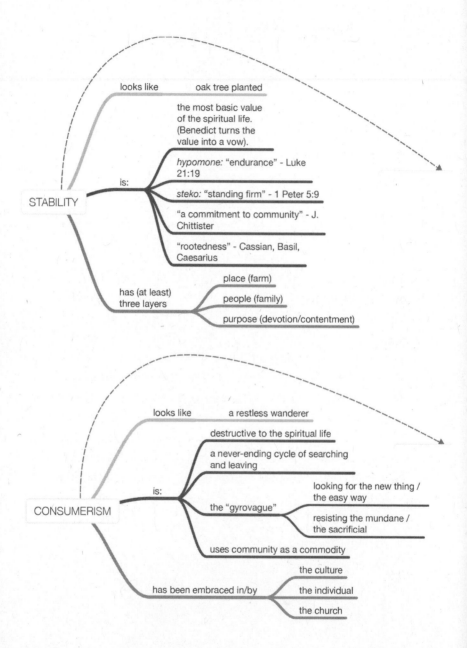

STABILITY

- looks like — oak tree planted
- is:
  - the most basic value of the spiritual life. (Benedict turns the value into a vow).
  - *hypomone:* "endurance" - Luke 21:19
  - *steko:* "standing firm" - 1 Peter 5:9
  - "a commitment to community" - J. Chittister
  - "rootedness" - Cassian, Basil, Caesarius
- has (at least) three layers
  - place (farm)
  - people (family)
  - purpose (devotion/contentment)

CONSUMERISM

- looks like — a restless wanderer
- is:
  - destructive to the spiritual life
  - a never-ending cycle of searching and leaving
  - the "gyrovague"
    - looking for the new thing / the easy way
    - resisting the mundane / the sacrificial
  - uses community as a commodity
- has been embraced in/by
  - the culture
  - the individual
  - the church

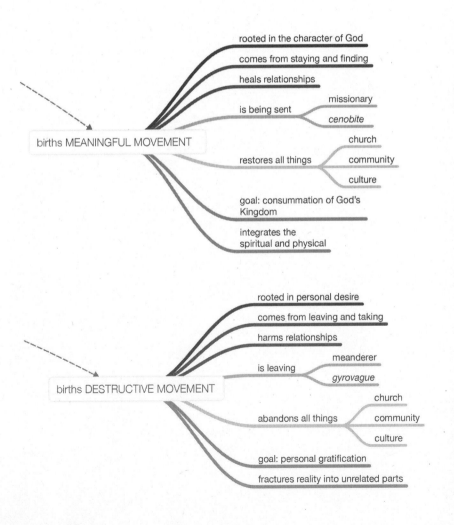

births MEANINGFUL MOVEMENT
- rooted in the character of God
- comes from staying and finding
- heals relationships
- is being sent
  - missionary
  - *cenobite*
- restores all things
  - church
  - community
  - culture
- goal: consummation of God's Kingdom
- integrates the spiritual and physical

births DESTRUCTIVE MOVEMENT
- rooted in personal desire
- comes from leaving and taking
- harms relationships
- is leaving
  - meanderer
  - *gyrovague*
- abandons all things
  - church
  - community
  - culture
- goal: personal gratification
- fractures reality into unrelated parts

ACKNOWLEDGMENTS

What a joy to review the last several years of work and the contributions of so many good people who helped bring this project to life!

I'm indebted to the Louisville Institute for the generous study grant and to Emmaus Church Community for the summer sabbatical. The gift of funds and time enabled me to visit several monastic communities and Benedict-influenced churches in the US and Italy.

Thanks to my dear friend Dr. Greg Thompson for helping me focus this project and for beautifully articulating both the theological foundation and the daily practice of stability. Greg graciously shared hours of conversation and introduced me to staff at Trinity Presbyterian Church in Charlottesville, who offered helpful insights and clarifying questions.

I'm grateful for my longtime friend Sister Maximilian Marie, OP, for encouraging my love for St. Benedict and for the introduction which led to a wonderful summer in Italy and a life-changing multi-week stay at the Monastero di San Benedetto in Monte in Norcia.

To Fr. Cassian, Fr. Benedict, Fr. Martin, and the brothers at the monastery, especially Br. Augustine and Br. Bernard, thank you. Your generous welcome and sincere love for our Lord continues to inspire my devotion to Jesus.

I'm thankful for friends Clint Nelson, Rich Lester, Rabbi Joshua Rubenstein, Dr. David McDonald, and Josh Unfried for questions, insights, sermons, and songs which contributed to this project.

Thanks to Dr. Stephen Campbell, who offered valuable feedback on my first draft, and to Rev. Steve Scott and fellow Sacramento District pastors for the encouraging opportunity to teach an early version of this material.

I'm grateful for space to write provided by Camp Alta, Mercy Center Auburn, and Papa's Barn.

Thanks to my mentor, Rev. Dr. Lyle Dorset, the first to encourage me to write, and to Dr. Jerry Root for believing in me enough to recommend this book.

Huge thanks to Jon Sweeney for believing in this project and for his careful editing, and to the team at Paraclete Press for making this book a reality.

Thanks to my longtime spiritual director, Fr. Thomas Brindley, who read grant proposals, wrote reference letters, helped me understand the relationship between the monastery and the church, and most importantly, continues to shepherd me and guide my growing love for St. Benedict and monasticism.

To our staff team, Rich and Melissa Lester, Angela Henning, Courtney Alves, and the whole Emmaus Church Community: thank you for joining me on this journey and for being the people and the place which have made our practice of stability so real and so rewarding.

I'm deeply grateful for my parents, whose marriage and home enabled me to experience stability decades before I ever read about it.

I'm so thankful to St. Benedict who, through his Rule, has become a guide and a friend.

And finally, to my family, my deepest thanks for your encouragement, sacrifice, and support as I've studied, traveled, and spent so many hours writing. Carmen, Sienna, Isaiah, and Matthias, you are my monastery. Your belief in me is fuel for my soul. I love you.

NOTES

1   Freddy Derwahl, *The Last Monk of Tibhirine: A True Story of Martyrdom, Faith, and Survival* (Brewster, MA: Paraclete Press, 2013), 106.

2   Timelines.ws cites *Wall Street Journal,* 7/11/96, p. A10.

3   John W. Kiser, *The Monks of Tibhirine: Faith, Love, and Terror in Algeria* (New York: St. Martin's Griffin, 2002), 205.

4   Kiser, *The Monks of Tibhirine,* 216.

5   Kiser, *The Monks of Tibhirine,* 221–22.

6   This scene, which I imagined was a dramatized summary of several conversations, is confirmed to have happened nearly exactly as depicted in the film *Of Gods and Men.* See also Kiser, *The Monks of Tibhirine,* 163.

7   Social holiness was an emphasis in the preaching of John Wesley, who believed the Christian call to holiness extended beyond personal piety to include "the transformation of the economic and political order, the establishment of Pentecostal commun(al)ism and the abolition of war." Theodore W. Jennings, Jr. *Good News to the Poor: John Wesley's Evangelical Economics* (Nashville: Abingdon Press, 1990), 153.

8   Quoted in Kiser, *The Monks of Tibhirine,* 207.

9   " *'stabilitas in congregatione'* describes the proper context for the instruments of spiritual progress. . . . We are rooted in a given community more than in a given place." Terrence Kardong, *Benedict's Rule* (Collegeville, MN: Liturgical Press, 1996), 473.

10   Timothy Fry, OSB, editor, *The Rule of St. Benedict in English* (Collegeville, MN: Liturgical Press, 1982), Prologue, v. 50. All quotations from the *Rule* of St. Benedict are from this translation.

11   Most significantly, from the Rule of the Master.

12   See volume 2 of Gregory's "Dialogues" called "The Life of St. Benedict." And, Constant J. Mews, *Gregory the Great, the Rule of Benedict and Roman Liturgy: The Evolution of a Legend,* published in the *Journal of Medieval History,* Volume 37, 2011.

13   That is, a life in committed community. Benedict refers to the community as the *fraternal acies,* the communal battleline, emphasizing "the mutual aid of comrades who take responsibility for the salvation of one another . . . supporting each other in the deadly warfare against the ancient enemy." Kardong, *Benedict's Rule,* 44.

14   Georg Holzherr, OSB, *The Rule of Benedict* (Collegeville, MN: Liturgical Press, 2016), 56.

15   RB 1:11.

16 RB Prologue, v. 45.

17 Joan Chittister, *The Rule of St. Benedict: A Spirituality for the 21st Century* (New York: Crossroad, 1992), 250.

18 The Greek words are *hypomoné* as in Luke 21:19: By standing firm/ enduring you will gain life and *stēkō*, "For now we really live, since you are standing firm in the Lord" (1 Thess. 3:8). "Resist him, standing firm in the faith, because you know that the family of believers throughout the world is undergoing the same kind of sufferings"(1 Pet. 5:9).

19 I love both this phrase and this powerful insight from Hubert van Zeller, *The Holy Rule* (New York: Sheed and Ward, 1958), 23, 370.

20 Thanks to Fr. Martin at Monastero di San Benedetto in Norcia for this phrase.

21 See, for example Exodus 6:7, Leviticus 26:12, Jeremiah 30:22, 2 Corinthians 6:16, Revelation 21:3.

22 See Genesis 12:2–3.

23 There are several examples of people who are leaving but are met by or stopped by or confronted by God. See the stories of Hagar in Genesis 16, Saul in Acts 9, Cleopas and his companion in Luke 24, for example.

24 "When the believing community is gathered by the Holy Spirit, and taught by the Spirit's gifts to live in charity and humility with one another and thus forming a particular monastic church, the Liturgy of the Hours makes present and acting the saving mystery of Christ." Francis Kline, *Lovers of the Place* (Collegeville, MN: Liturgical Press, 1997), 41.

25 Thanks to Kathleen Norris, who uses the phrase "settle down and allow God to find us where we are" in her introduction to Jonathan Wilson-Hartgrove's *The Wisdom of Stability: Rooting Faith in a Mobile Culture* (Brewster, MA: Paraclete Press, 2010), ix.

26 Thanks to my dear friend Dr. Greg Thompson for this phrase.

27 Chittister, *The Rule of St. Benedict*, 247.

28 Again, credit the warrior-poet Dr. Greg Thompson.

29 Nicholas Buxton, *The Oblate Life*, ed. Gervase Holdaway, OSB (Collegeville, MN: Liturgical Press, 2008), 161.

30 Rule of St. Benedict 4:78, 58:9, and 58:17.

31 Buxton: *The Oblate Life*, 160.

32 Esther de Waal, *Seeking God: The Way of St. Benedict* (Collegeville, MN: Liturgical Press, 1984), 55.

33 de Waal, *Seeking God*, 60, 58.

34 RB Prologue 47.

35 Kathleen Norris, *The Cloister Walk* (New York: Riverhead, 1997), 14.

36 de Waal, *Seeking God*, 62.

37 de Waal, *Seeking God*, 62.

38 Milena Jesenská, "The Art of Standing Still," quoted in Kiser, *The Monks of Tibhirine*, 156.

39 RB, Prologue, v. 1.

40 RB 35:1, 22:8, 63, 63:17 and Romans 12:10; RB 72:5, 72:6, 72:7.

41 van Zeller, *The Holy Rule*, 104.

42 From the introduction to Kline, *Lovers of the Place*, vi.

43 Thanks to Jonathan Wilson-Hartgrove and his book *The Wisdom of Stability* for help with this insight.

44 Kline, *Lovers of the Place*, 85.

45 Credit and deep gratitude to my spiritual director, Fr. Thomas Brindley, who has served as a faithful guide to me for more than 20 years.

46 Benedicta Ward, *The Desert Fathers* (New York: Penguin Books, 2003), 72.

47 Ward, *The Desert Fathers*, 72.

48 Quote taken from the January 30, 2020, Instagram post by @pete_k_muller. Emphasis mine.

49 de Waal, *Seeking God*, 56–57.

50 RB 1:11.

51 My summary of Wilson-Hartgrove, *The Wisdom of Stability*, 40–41.

52 de Waal, *Seeking God*, 56–57.

53 Margaret Guenther, *My Soul in Silence Waits* (Cambridge, MA: Cowley, 2000), 21.

54 Guenther includes these questions "for prayer and pondering" at the end of her chapter on Longing: "What do I want, truly want? What desires have I suppressed or denied? Why? What do I love, truly love? How would I order these loves? What is merely liking or attraction? What can I let go of easily? What should I let go of? What are the loves that define and sustain me?" (p. 31).

55 Quoted from the January 27, 2020, Instagram post of National Geographic photographer @pete_k_muller.

56 Quoted from the January 30, 2020, Instagram post of National Geographic photographer @pete_k_muller.

57 Thomas Merton, *The Sign of Jonas* (New York: Harvest Book, 1953), 63.

58 *Of Gods and Men* is a 2010 French film directed by Xavier Beauvois.

59 Credit Wade Bradshaw, Pastor of Spiritual Formation at Trinity Church in Charlottesville, Virginia, for sharing this powerful insight with me during a conversation on May 2, 2018.

60 Merton, *The Sign of Jonas*, 34.

61 Stan Ingersol, *Nazarene Roots, Pastors, Prophets, Revivalists, Reformers* (Kansas City, MO: Beacon Hill Press, 2009), 90.

62 The Manual of the Church of the Nazarene (Kansas City, MO: Beacon Hill Press), 18.

63 "There is no holiness but social holiness" is a quote commonly attributed to John Wesley.

64 Matthew 6:10.

65 Christian de Chergé, remembering and then reflecting on the words of his friend Gilles Nicolas, in Kiser, *The Monks of Tibhirine*, 217.

66 Eugene Peterson's translation of John 1:14.

67 M. Raymond, OCSO, from the introduction to *The Family that overtook Christ* (Dublin: Clonmore and Reynolds, 1944), quoted in de Waal, *Seeking God*, 25.

68 van Zeller, *The Holy Rule*, 23.

69 Thanks to Marva J. Dawn's book *A Royal Waste of Time: The Splendor of Worshiping God and Being Church for the World* (Grand Rapids, MI: Eerdmans, 1999), 2.

70 Psalm 131:1–2.

71 From a conversation with Brother B., summer 2018.

72 RB 43:3.

ABOUT PARACLETE PRESS

PARACLETE PRESS is the publishing arm of the Cape Cod monastic community, the Community of Jesus. Presenting a full expression of Christian belief and practice, we reflect the ecumenical charism of the Community and its dedication to sacred music, the fine arts, and the written word.

Learn more about us at our website
www.paracletepress.com
or phone us toll-free at 1.800.451.5006

SCAN
TO
READ
MORE

YOU MAY ALSO BE INTERESTED IN THESE...

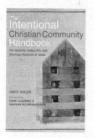
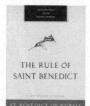